GOODMAN FOR ARCHITECTS

American philosopher Nelson Goodman (1906–1998) was one of the foremost analytic thinkers of the twentieth century, with groundbreaking contributions in the fields of logic, philosophy of science, epistemology, and aesthetics. This book is an introduction to the main aspects of Goodman's philosophy as they relate to architecture and the built environment.

Goodman specifically discussed architecture in his major work on aesthetics, *The Languages of Art: An Approach to a Theory of Symbols* (1968), and in two essays 'How Buildings Mean' (1985), and 'On Capturing Cities' (1991). His main philosophical notions in *Ways of Worldmaking* (1978) also apply well to architecture. Goodman's thought is particularly attractive because of its constructive aspect: there is not a given and immutable world, but both knowledge and reality are constantly built and rebuilt. Whereas other theories, such as deconstruction, implicitly entail an undoing of modern precepts, Goodman's conception of world-making offers a positive, constructive way to understand how a plural reality is made and remade.

Goodman's approach to architecture is not only relevant thinking in providing new insights to understanding the built environment, but also serves as an illustration of analytic thinking in architecture. This book shows that the methods, concepts, and ways of arguing characteristic of analytic philosophy are helpful tools to examine buildings in a novel and fruitful way, and they will certainly enhance the architect's critical skills when designing and thinking about architecture.

Remei Capdevila-Werning wrote her dissertation on Goodman and architecture and is a postdoctoral researcher at the Universitat Autònoma de Barcelona, Spain.

Thinkers for Architects

Series Editor: Adam Sharr, Newcastle University, UK

Editorial Board

Jonathan A. Hale, University of Nottingham, UK

Hilde Heynen, KU Leuven, Netherlands

David Leatherbarrow, University of Pennsylvania, USA

Architects have often looked to philosophers and theorists from beyond the discipline for design inspiration or in search of a critical framework for practice. This original series offers quick, clear introductions to key thinkers who have written about architecture and whose work can yield insights for designers.

'Each unintimidatingly slim book makes sense of the subjects' complex theories.'

Building Design

'... a valuable addition to any studio space or computer lab.'

Architectural Record

'... a creditable attempt to present their subjects in a useful way.'

Architectural Review

Deleuze and Guattari for Architects
Andrew Ballantyne

Heidegger for Architects
Adam Sharr

Irigaray for Architects
Peg Rawes

Bhabha for Architects
Felipe Hernández

Bourdieu for Architects
Helena Webster

Benjamin for Architects
Brian Elliott

Derrida for Architects
Richard Coyne

Gadamer for Architects
Jonathan Hale

Foucault for Architects
Gordana Fontana-Giusti

Goodman for Architects
Remei Capdevila-Werning

Virilio for Architects
John Armitage

THINKERS FOR ARCHITECTS

Goodman
for
Architects

Remei Capdevila-Werning

LONDON AND NEW YORK

First published 2014
by Routledge
2 Park Square, Milton Park, Abingdon, Oxon OX14 4RN

Simultaneously published in the USA and Canada
by Routledge
711 Third Avenue, New York, NY 10017

Routledge is an imprint of the Taylor & Francis Group, an informa business

© 2014 Remei Capdevila-Werning

The right of Remei Capdevila-Werning to be identified as author of this work has been asserted by her in accordance with sections 77 and 78 of the Copyright, Designs and Patents Act 1988.

All rights reserved. No part of this book may be reprinted or reproduced or utilised in any form or by any electronic, mechanical, or other means, now known or hereafter invented, including photocopying and recording, or in any information storage or retrieval system, without permission in writing from the publishers.

Trademark notice: Product or corporate names may be trademarks or registered trademarks, and are used only for identification and explanation without intent to infringe.

British Library Cataloguing in Publication Data
A catalogue record for this book is available from the British Library

Library of Congress Cataloging in Publication Data
Capdevila Werning, Remei.
Goodman for architects / Remei Capdevila Werning.
pages cm. -- (Thinkers for architects)
Includes bibliographical references and index.
1. Goodman, Nelson. 2. Architecture--Philosophy. I. Title.
B945.G624C37 2013
191--dc23
2013015506

ISBN: 978-0-415-63936-1 (hbk)
ISBN: 978-0-415-63937-8 (pbk)
ISBN: 978-1-315-88419-6 (ebk)

Typeset in Frutiger and Galliard
by Fakenham Prepress Solutions, Fakenham, Norfolk NR21 8NN

Printed and bound in Great Britain by
TJ International Ltd, Padstow, Cornwall

To Pete

Contents

Series Editor's Preface	xi
Acknowledgements	xiii
Illustrations Credits	xiv
1. Introduction	1
2. When is Architecture?	9

Essentialism and Goodman's account 10

Intentionalism and Goodman's account 14

Institutionalism and Goodman's account 19

Aesthetic experience of architecture 23

3. Buildings as Symbols	31

Symbol and symbol systems 31

Denotation 38

Exemplification 46

Articulation 53

Expression 54

Other modes of reference 65

    Allusion 65

    Variation 69

    Style 73

Evaluation and criteria of rightness 75

Again: When is architecture? The symptoms of the aesthetic 77

4. Identity of Architectural Works   80

Autographic and allographic 80
Architecture's notation 83
Between autographic and allographic 87
Autographic versus allographic: the Barcelona Pavilion 93

5. Buildings as Ways of Worldmaking   100

From epistemology to metaphysics: worldmaking 100
Architectural ways of worldmaking 104

For Further Reading   114
Bibliography   116
Index   121

Series Editor's Preface

Adam Sharr

Architects have often looked to thinkers in philosophy and theory for design ideas, or in search of a critical framework for practice. Yet architects and students of architecture can struggle to navigate thinkers' writings. It can be daunting to approach original texts with little appreciation of their contexts. And existing introductions seldom explore architectural material in any detail. This original series offers clear, quick, and accurate introductions to key thinkers who have written about architecture. Each book summarizes what a thinker has to offer for architects. It locates their architectural thinking in the body of their work, introduces significant books and essays, helps decode terms, and provides quick reference for further reading. If you find philosophical and theoretical writing about architecture difficult, or just don't know where to begin, this series will be indispensable.

Books in the *Thinkers for Architects* series come out of architecture. They pursue architectural modes of understanding, aiming to introduce a thinker to an architectural audience. Each thinker has a unique and distinctive ethos, and the structure of each book derives from the character at its focus. The thinkers explored are prodigious writers and any short introduction can only address a fraction of their work. Each author – an architect or an architectural critic – has focused on a selection of a thinker's writings which they judge most relevant to designers and interpreters of architecture. Inevitably, much will be left out. These books will be the first point of reference, rather than the last word, about a particular thinker for architects. It is hoped that they will encourage you to read further, offering an incentive to delve deeper into the original writings of a particular thinker.

The *Thinkers for Architects* series has proved highly successful, expanding now to ten volumes dealing with familiar cultural figures whose writings have influenced architectural designers, critics, and commentators in distinctive and important ways. Books explore the work of: Gilles Deleuze and Felix Guattari; Martin Heidegger; Luce Irigaray; Homi Bhabha; Pierre Bourdieu; Walter Benjamin; Jacques Derrida; Hans-Georg Gadamer, Michel Foucault, and Nelson Goodman. A number of future volumes are projected, addressing Jean Baudrillard, Paul Virilio, and Maurice Merleau-Ponty. The series continues to expand, addressing an increasingly rich diversity of contemporary thinkers who have something to say to architects.

Adam Sharr is Professor of Architecture at the University of Newcastle-upon-Tyne, Principal of Adam Sharr Architects, and Editor (with Richard Weston) of *arq: Architectural Research Quarterly*, a Cambridge University Press international architecture journal. His books published by Routledge include *Heidegger for Architects* and *Reading Architecture and Culture*.

Acknowledgements

This book would have not been possible without the support and encouragement of many people and institutions. Thanks to my family and friends, for being always there, and to my colleagues and professors who have been there in one stage or another of my work on Goodman and architecture. The research for this book received the financial support of several institutions. I am grateful for the various grants awarded by the Catalan Government, the Real Colegio Complutense Fellowship, and 'la Caixa' Fellowship for graduate studies in the United States.

Joan Capdevila, Keta Capdevila-Werning, Razan Francis, Jèssica Jaques, Andrea Merrett, Josep Montserrat, Peter Oberschelp, Gerard Vilar, and Sigrid Werning have provided insightful comments and suggestions to earlier versions of this book. Many thanks to all of them. Special thanks to Catherine Z. Elgin and to Lydia Goehr, for their continuous support and guidance, critical insights, and invaluable knowledge.

I am grateful to Routledge's Georgina Johnson-Cook, Fran Ford, and Laura Williamson, for accompanying me throughout the publication process. Thanks also to the editor of the series, Adam Sharr, and to Routledge, for believing in the importance of introducing an analytic thinker to the 'Thinkers for Architects' series and for letting that be Goodman.

Finally, my deepest gratitude and love to my husband, Peter Minosh, whose constant encouragement, patience, and challenging thinking about architecture make things worthwhile. I dedicate this book to him.

Remei Capdevila-Werning
New York, Winter 2013

Illustration credits

Remei Capdevila-Werning, pages 44, 45, 94

Catherine Z. Elgin, page xv

The Landmark Trust, page 60

Peter Minosh, pages 26, 45, 51, 91

Jordi Pons Pagès, page 36

RCR Arquitectes, page 35

Anna Vila Espuña, page 62

Nelson Goodman.

CHAPTER 1

Introduction

Analytic philosophy, characterized by its rigorous and detail-centred methods and argumentation, provides an approach to architecture that complements the variety of theories that architects are already acquainted with and enhances their critical skills for both designing and thinking about architecture. While there is no doubt about the significant influence of continental philosophy on architectural thought (with contributions by thinkers such as Benjamin, Deleuze, Derrida, Foucault, or Heidegger), Anglo-American analytic philosophy also provides a relevant account of architecture that should no longer be disregarded. Nelson Goodman provides such an account. His philosophy is exemplary of analytic thinking and, most importantly, provides a fruitful and compelling way to reflect about architecture and the built environment. The present book thus introduces Goodman's philosophy as applied to architecture and shows the unique role that architecture plays in both the creation of meaning and the making of reality.

As one of the foremost analytic philosophers of the twentieth century, Goodman made groundbreaking contributions to almost all philosophical disciplines, from logic and philosophy of science, to metaphysics, epistemology, and aesthetics, where his reflections on architecture are found. This wide range constitutes, as will be shown, a cohesive whole characterized by constructivist, relativist, irrealist, and pluralist philosophical convictions. Throughout Goodman's work, there is thus a leading thread that is best illustrated by his major publications. It starts with his dissertation, *A Study of Qualities* (1941), which constitutes the basis of his first book, *The Structure of Appearance* (1951), continues with *Fact, Fiction, and Forecast* (1954), *Languages of Art: An Approach to a Theory of Symbols* (1968), *Problems and Projects* (1972), *Ways of Worldmaking* (1978), *Of Mind and Other Matters* (1984), and ends with *Reconceptions in Philosophy and Other Arts and Sciences* (1988, co-authored

1   INTRODUCTION

with Catherine Z. Elgin). Goodman specifically examines architecture in his major work on aesthetics, *Languages of Art,* and in two essays entitled 'How Buildings Mean' (1985, later published in *Reconceptions*), and 'On Capturing Cities' (1991). His main philosophical notions and theses apply as well to architecture, especially those discussed in *Ways of Worldmaking*.

Goodman was not prone to talking about himself. In the *Fiftieth anniversary report* of Harvard University Class of 1928, Goodman includes among his aversions 'writing anything autobiographical like this', 'this' being a short updated biography about his career and whereabouts (Harvard College, Class of 1928, 1978: 260). This statement reflects his unwillingness to look back, and rather indicates his desire 'to look forward to the next philosophical problem or work of art' (Elgin 2000: 2). A brief note on his life, which spanned most of the twentieth century, may nevertheless be useful. Born in Somerville, Massachusetts on 7 August, 1906, Henry Nelson Goodman attended Harvard University, receiving a B.S. in 1928 and a Ph.D. in Philosophy in 1941. During his graduate studies, he was running the Goodman-Walker Art Gallery in Boston, a way to sustain himself due to the impossibility of getting any fellowships because of his Jewish origins. This is how he became acquainted with art and started his own extensive collection (some of Goodman's artworks are currently at the Harvard Art Museums, where he bequeathed them, and are accessible online through Harvard's library catalogue). At the gallery he also met artist Katharine Sturgis, whom he married in 1944. He served the US Army during World War II as a psychological tester and afterwards he began his academic career, first at Tufts University (1945–6), then at the University of Pennsylvania (1946–64), at Brandeis University (1964–7), to end up again at Harvard, where he taught from 1968 to his retirement in 1977, when he became emeritus Professor. Apart from his philosophical work, Goodman was interested in the arts in a non-theoretical way: in addition to collecting and running an art gallery, he founded the Harvard Summer Dance Program and Project Zero at Harvard Graduate School of Education, an interdisciplinary program for research in education and the arts; he also commissioned, produced, and directed the artistic performances *Hockey Seen, Rabbit Run*, and *Variations: An Illustrated Lecture Concert*. He continued working actively in various projects, until his death on 25 November, 1998, at age 92, in Needham, Massachusetts. (A more extensive biography and a summary of Goodman's main contributions is in Elgin *et al.* 1999, Carter 2000, and Elgin 2000).

Following Goodman's philosophy, architecture's task does not simply entail the physical construction of buildings that fulfil practical functions, but is also an active participation to the creation of meaning and reality. Architecture has therefore an epistemological role, insofar as it contributes to the making of meaning and understanding, and a metaphysical role, insofar as it contributes the making of reality and the world beyond just assembling materials. On the one hand, architecture creates meaning and contributes to the advancement of our understanding in a unique manner. This contribution is as valid as the ones conveyed by any other discipline, from sciences to humanities, from arts to everyday life, and there is no pre-established hierarchy that privileges one over the others: the meaning provided by science, for instance, is not superior or better than the one provided by architecture. Epistemology is hence concerned with all sorts of meaning; understanding is not limited to propositional knowledge, i.e., the one expressed by declarative sentences, but is a much broader notion that includes all sorts of beliefs, opinions, emotions, and experiences. What one learns from architecture, be it a conception of space, the building's features, or something about oneself is not knowledge, but understanding. For Goodman, these meanings provided by architecture are irreducible to knowledge or other kinds of understanding. What we gain when experiencing a building cannot be completely transposed into words; it can be described through propositional knowledge, but something gets lost in translation. Architecture, thus, enhances understanding in a distinctive way.

Following Goodman's philosophy, architecture's task does not simply entail the physical construction of buildings that fulfil practical functions, but is also an active participation to the creation of meaning and reality.

Within this epistemological framework, buildings convey meaning by symbolizing. Or, better, buildings are symbols that mean many things in various ways. A farm may refer to a kind of dwelling, an economic activity, traditional values, an architectural style, or nostalgia for a way of life in decline. A parliament building may stand for political values, one of the nation's pillars, or it may ironically stand for the false pretence of democracy in a corrupt country. A church symbolizes a particular religion, style, period, grandeur, solace, or its structure and construction materials. As symbols, buildings bear interpretation. To find out what they mean, we need to interpret them according to the symbol systems to which they belong, for symbols do not function in isolation. A house symbolizes a certain style within a system that classifies buildings according to stylistic features; it symbolizes being a residential building within a system that classifies buildings according to the activities they shelter; it symbolizes its size and distribution, but not its furniture or wall colour within a system that sorts out the features a house has to display as a model house. This might seem an unusual process, but we are constantly learning how symbol systems work and interpreting symbols: from languages to mathematical formulas, from traffic lights to works of art, from gestures to constellations. We live surrounded by symbols, creating and interpreting them. Accordingly, by designing and erecting buildings, architects are also symbol-makers.

On the other hand, architecture's contribution to the creation of meaning and the advancement of understanding has its metaphysical counterpart, which is that of making worlds in a fundamental sense. By symbolizing, architecture participates in the process of worldmaking. Buildings may refer many things under different symbol systems which are irreducible to one another; there are hence various symbol systems that lack a last referent that would serve as their common ground. For Goodman, this means that the plurality of symbol systems corresponds to a plurality of worlds, each of them irreducible to the others. In other words, it is not the case that there is one world and many interpretations of it, but rather that these various interpretations and meanings actually constitute different worlds. As symbols are constantly made and remade, interpreted and reinterpreted starting from previous symbols and symbol systems, worlds are also constantly made and remade, constructed and reconstructed starting from previous worlds or world-versions. This is why Goodman's philosophy is characterized as pluralist, constructivist, irrealist, and relativist. This is also why for Goodman epistemology and metaphysics meet, because the various construals of the world are at the same time constructions of the world. Buildings are not just physical objects and, as such, constitutive elements of the world, but rather every construal of a building contributes to worldmaking. Given this interrelation with meaning and reality and architecture's central role in both, the task of the architect acquires a wider significance as the task of designing results in the very creation of meaning as well as of worlds. In Goodman's terms, architects are primarily world-makers.

We live surrounded by symbols, creating and interpreting them. Accordingly, by designing and erecting buildings, architects are also symbol-makers.

Goodman's discussion on architecture takes place within aesthetics, which means that architecture is considered as an art. Works of art and architecture are symbols with particular characteristics. When a building serves solely to shelter a practical function, it does not symbolize, it is just a building; when it symbolizes in an aesthetic or artistic way, then it is architecture. And when it symbolizes in a non-aesthetic way, in a political or religious manner, for instance, it is a symbol, but not architecture. What a construction is depends on (and is relative to) its symbolic functioning. It is not the case that a building is architecture because its creator intended to do so, because it was designed to be architecture, or because the historical, social, and institutional context so determines. Rather, the status of a building is a matter of how it is interpreted. Thus Goodman's question of 'when is art?', or here, of 'when is architecture?' does not address architecture's temporal status, but the conditions under which one and the same building can simultaneously be just a building, architecture, or a symbol of another sort.

In Goodman's terms, architects are primarily world-makers.

Given that works of art and architecture are symbols, their main role is cognitive; they are characterized above all by their capacity of creating and conveying meaning and not by their beauty or their capacity to awaken emotions, for example. Our engagement with works of art and architecture is not a passive reception, but an active process of discerning and interpreting a work's meanings. Aesthetics is thus an integral part of epistemology and, since through the creation and interpretation of symbols worlds are made, aesthetics is also an integral part of metaphysics. That architecture is considered as an art and examined as an artistic symbol does not mean that the theory of symbols only applies to buildings when functioning as art. Goodman's theory of symbols is concerned with any sort of symbol and this is precisely what creates a common ground for all sorts of understanding and also the several worlds to whose making they contribute. Architecture's social, cultural, and political meanings can also be understood in symbol theoretical terms, which entails that buildings do not only contribute to artistic worlds, but can participate to the creation of any kind of world. Since buildings may be part of multiple symbol systems and worlds, architects have an enormous potential for construing and reconstruing, constructing and reconstructing all of them.

Goodman's theory of symbols is concerned with any sort of symbol and this is precisely what creates a common ground for all sorts of understanding and also the several worlds to whose making they contribute.

This book is structured following the conceptual development just described. Chapter 2 deals with the question of 'when is architecture?'. By asking 'when' rather than 'what', architecture is examined within a relativist conceptual framework that considers that buildings are symbols. This explains the fact that buildings may sometimes be architecture and sometimes not and offers a solution to problems that three different approaches to architecture fail to solve: an essentialist account, which maintains that there are essential properties that determine what architecture is; an intentionalist account, according to which the intentions (generally of the architect) determine what counts as architecture; and an institutionalist account, which defends that what architecture is is decided by a series of established institutions and groups of experts. This chapter further discusses aesthetic experience in architecture, for the process of interpreting buildings as artistic symbols occurs when aesthetically experiencing a work. Chapter 3, 'Buildings as Symbols', examines how symbolization takes place in architecture. It explains Goodman's conceptions of symbol and symbol systems, discusses the various modes of reference (denotation, exemplification, expression, allusion, variation, and style), and presents articulation as a means to prompt symbolization in buildings. Evaluation and criteria of rightness of both symbolization and interpretation are also addressed in this chapter, which finishes by answering again the initial question of 'when is architecture' by identifying the so-called symptoms of the aesthetic, a response that can only be given once Goodman's theory of symbols has been discussed. Chapter 4 addresses issues of identity of architectural works. While certain buildings are considered as originals and others as their copies, other buildings are considered as instances of the same work and yet other buildings, such as restored structures and reconstructions, are hybrid cases. Goodman's notions of the autographic and the allographic serve as conceptual tools to philosophically explain these differences. Within this context, architecture's notation (constituted by plans, elevations, and sections) acquires a role of establishing the identity of allographic works. Finally, Chapter 5 examines how buildings contribute to the making and remaking of worlds. It explains the transition from symbolization to worldmaking and the underlying metaphysical assumptions that constitute Goodman's constructivist, pluralist, and relativist thinking. The discussion of specific architectural examples shows architecture's distinct involvement in the process of worldmaking.

There are plenty of examples throughout the book. This is not only for pedagogic purposes, but because for Goodman examples play a central role in both understanding and developing a theory. Examples are symbols that, as their name indicates, exemplify certain properties, and they do so in a way that is not completely transposable to other sorts of symbols. Good examples provide a privileged epistemic access to properties and concepts that otherwise would remain obscure. Developing one's own examples and counter-examples is an important way of developing arguments, thinking, and reflecting. Therefore, everyone is invited to find their own examples to think and reflect about architecture.

CHAPTER 2

When is Architecture?

Some constructions are generally considered to be architecture and others not: 'A bicycle shed is a building; Lincoln Cathedral is a piece of architecture' (Pevsner 1963: 15). Likewise, the Taj Mahal is a work of architecture while the apartment block where I live is simply a building. No matter whether one agrees or not, whether these distinctions are elitist or controversial, 'whether they arise … from the stomach or the imagination' (Marx 1990: 125), it is not an uncommon classification that requires closer examination. Similarly, certain structures are sometimes works of architecture under certain circumstances but not under others: saltbox houses, among the earliest New England homes, had a primary function of providing shelter and now many of them are taken as artistic examples of American colonial architecture. And yet in other cases works of architecture can become simply buildings under other conditions, as happened to the first skyscrapers when their novelty and exceptionality became the norm. How can these shifts be explained? How can the change in a building's stature be philosophically accounted for? Goodman addresses this issue when posing the question of 'When is art?' or, here, the question of 'When is architecture?'.

> **Part of the trouble lies in asking the wrong question – in failing to recognize that a thing may function as a work of art at some time and not at others. In crucial cases, the real question is not 'What objects are (permanently) works of art?' but 'When is an object a work of art?' – or more briefly, as in my title, 'When is art?'**
>
> **(Goodman 1978: 66–7)**

Goodman proposes this functional approach to art and architecture in a central chapter of his *Ways of Worldmaking*, precisely entitled 'When Is Art?'. Since, for Goodman, no satisfactory answers have been given to the question about the essence of art and architecture, a change in focus may be helpful to understand not what architecture is, but rather when a construction functions as architecture and in that way explain how it is possible that one and the same building can be architecture in some cases and not in others. This shifting from 'what' to 'when', thus, is not simply a word game: it enables a completely different approach to architecture that abandons an essentialist take in favour of a much broader and elastic characterization, which for Goodman is a constructivist and functional one. This change in the question is what leads one to consider that buildings are symbols. Moreover, by changing the approach, the essentialist, intentionalist, and institutionalist accounts of architecture are rejected and the difficulties they pose are resolved. This chapter discusses these three accounts and introduces the fundamentals of Goodman's philosophy while explaining how his account addresses issues that other approaches fail to solve.

Essentialism and Goodman's account

An essentialist account of architecture aims to formulate the necessary properties that make something be architecture; it aims to provide a definition of what architecture is. As it turns out, however, it is quite difficult and problematic to determine exactly what the essence of architecture is and, consequently, to provide an adequate definition. Consider a standard definition of architecture as it is found in the *Oxford English Dictionary* (*OED*). Here, the first entry states that architecture is '[t]he art or science of building or constructing edifices of any kind for human use'. Contrasting this specific definition with the current use of the term 'architecture', one realizes that this definition is either too limiting or too broad: it excludes, for instance, landscape architecture as well as all buildings not intended 'for human use', such as poultry yards, pigsties, silos, warehouses, temples to the gods, obelisks, or garden follies. Although each of these kinds of constructions can indeed be designated as an architectural work, they are left out of the aforementioned definition, for the essential properties it includes ('building or constructing edifices' and 'for human use') are too limiting and excluding. Furthermore, the *OED* definition overlooks the distinction usually made between some constructions that are architecture and others that are simply buildings: we consider that the Taj Mahal is a work of architecture but the apartment building where I live is not. Thus in this sense the definition is too broad. One could try to amend the initial definition by extending and refining it, as is actually done in the *OED*: 'But architecture is sometimes regarded solely as a fine art.' In that way, the difference between simple buildings and works of architecture is acknowledged, although the issue of finding an exact definition and therefore the essential properties of architecture is not solved. Rather, it is only deferred towards finding an exact definition of the other terms that constitute architecture's definition, such as 'fine art'. Despite this enhancement, the definition of architecture would continue being incomplete. We could continue adapting and rewriting this definition until it could seem that it covers all the cases we properly consider as architecture. However hard we would try, though, there could always be a case that obliges us to modify the definition and, therefore, the undertaking of giving a definition becomes a Sisyphean task.

Apart from the impossibility of providing a perfect and ultimate definition that would comprise all of the architectural works of the past, present, and future (among other reasons, because of the continuous innovation and evolution of architecture), the essentialist definition of architecture does not explain how one and the same building can be a work of architecture under certain circumstances and not under others. The same saltbox house can be understood both as an architectural work and just as a place to provide shelter; it is not the case that saltbox houses become works of architecture and thus suddenly gain an essential feature they did not have before, which causes a change in their stature, or that we recognize that they had always been architectural works and we had been misconceiving them. Saltbox houses remain essentially the same. An essentialist definition of architecture is unable to explain such transformations because essentialism is rigid: one can enhance or reduce the definition by adding or eliminating essential properties whenever it would seem necessary, but this could never include the cases that are not permanently, but rather temporarily, works of architecture; it could never include, either, buildings that can be simultaneously considered as works of architecture and simply as buildings.

Apart from the impossibility of providing a perfect and ultimate definition that would comprise all of the architectural works of the past, present, and future (among other reasons, because of the continuous innovation and evolution of architecture), the essentialist definition of architecture does not explain how one and the same building can be a work of architecture under certain circumstances and not under others.

To overcome all these difficulties posed by an essentialist account, Goodman proposes asking 'when' instead of 'what' and responds by characterizing architecture from a functional perspective. When, then, is architecture? Architecture is when a building functions as a work of art. Or, to put it in a grammatically correct form, a building is a work of architecture when it functions as a work of art. There are buildings that never function as a work of architecture – my apartment building; some that have functioned as architecture since their completion – the Taj Mahal; buildings that may become architecture and function as such at a certain point – saltbox houses; buildings that functioned as architecture but ceased functioning as such – the first skyscrapers; and buildings that sometimes function as architecture and sometimes not, as is the case of any building that fulfils a practical function and can also be considered as a work of architecture. The subsequent question to ask is how it is possible that a building functions sometimes as architecture and sometimes not. Goodman responds:

> My answer is that just as an object may be a symbol ... at certain times and under certain circumstances and not at others, so an object may be a work

of art at some times and not at others. Indeed, just by virtue of functioning as a symbol in a certain way does an object become, while so functioning, a work of art.

(Goodman 1978: 67)

A work of art or architecture is a symbol with particular characteristics.

In this excerpt we find a key notion of Goodman's philosophy: symbol. In the broadest sense, something is a symbol when it refers to or stands for something; symbolization, or reference, is thus a 'relation between a symbol and whatever it stands for in any way' (Goodman 1988: 124). A symbol requires interpretation to determine what it means. A work of art or architecture is a symbol with particular characteristics. There are many kinds of symbols, but an object is an artistic or aesthetic symbol only when its referential functioning fulfils certain conditions. A building may just be a building that does not symbolize at all; it can also be a symbol, but not necessarily an artistic symbol. Just as there are many kinds of symbols, symbols can mean various things in different ways, and for this reason they bear interpretation. A courthouse may be a symbol of justice, but also of fear and respect; a church may stand for piety, but also grandiosity and calmness; a skyscraper may symbolize economic power and technological progress; a specific hospital may symbolize protection and cure, but also happiness or sadness, depending on the experience one had in that place; the university building can be a symbol for humanity's accumulated wisdom, for freedom of thought, for advancement of understanding, and can also refer to the best years of one's life or maybe the worst ones. Buildings can symbolize social values, personal incidents, cultural and historical episodes by an associative process, and this symbolic functioning is not aesthetic. Goodman defines the aesthetic functioning of buildings as follows:

A building is a work of art only insofar as it signifies, means, refers, symbolizes in some way.

(Goodman 1988: 33)

To function as an aesthetic symbol, i.e., to be a work of architecture, a building has to be a symbol of a certain sort, has to symbolize in determinate ways different from the other non-aesthetic symbols, which means that it has to function within an artistic symbol system, as is discussed in the next chapter. The important issue at this point is that, if buildings are symbols, then it can be explained how they can simultaneously be works of architecture and just buildings while avoiding essentialist queries. If buildings are symbols, it can also be explained why an intentionalist account of architecture is also inadequate in providing a definition of architecture.

Intentionalism and Goodman's account

According to an intentionalist account, something is a work of architecture if its creator intended it to be so. Intentionalism maintains that the work's definition is based on the relation between creator and object and that the work's meaning depends on the creator's intentions. So, if I intend to build an architectural work honouring my ancestors, the outcome of this intention will be nothing more nor less than a work of architecture honouring my ancestors. This is a simplified characterization of intentionalism: the advocates of this account do not always agree on what intentions are or on what role they play and attribute to them different degrees of relevance in art (Iseminger 1992 and Kieran 2006 provide an introduction to intentionalism in art). This characterization, however, suffices to explain Goodman's reasons to reject intentionalism when both providing a definition of architecture and determining what a building means. Goodman disagrees that intentions can completely determine what constitutes an architectural work and its meaning. If the architect's intentions were the only thing that mattered, then there would only be one right interpretation of a work, whose content would be the author's intentions regarding the work and its meaning. Goodman rejects this absolutist view (Goodman 1988: 44) and, instead, maintains that the architect's intention is just one interpretation with no pre-eminent value in respect to any other possible interpretations of the work. There are several reasons to support this rejection and hence to refute an intentionalist account.

Goodman disagrees that intentions can completely determine what constitutes an architectural work and its meaning.

First, it is not always possible to know the artist's intention or intentions when creating the work, as happens with anonymous works: we do not know who built the Romanesque churches at the Vall de Boí (in the Catalan Pyrenees) or the exact purpose of their creator or creators. If the only possible and correct interpretation of a work were based on the creator's intentions, then no further interpretations would be valid; better yet, there would be no way to know whether any of our interpretations were correct, for we would not be able to contrast them with the creator's intention or interpretation. And this is not the case: there are plenty of interpretations of the churches at the Vall de Boí and we do have criteria to evaluate these interpretations. Furthermore, there is the problem of determining which among the creator's intentions is valid: the first intention when designing the work, the one when building it, just after finishing it, or many years after, to mention only a few. This problem of determining the creator's intentions is even more complicated in architecture, because many people intervene in the construction process and one cannot assume that all of them share the same intentions. Note that Goodman does not question the existence of intentions; he questions that we can have access to the intentions the artist or architect had when creating the work and that we can determine which specific intention is relevant to both the work's meaning and its definition, which brings him to reject an intentionalist account of architecture and art.

Second, works of art may arise from unintended results that have nothing to do with the creator's initial intentions, thus making intentions irrelevant to determine what a work of architecture is. Most of the chimneys of the factories in the Poblenou neighbourhood of Barcelona were built solely with functional intentions. This functional necessity, however, produced an artistic outcome, which allows us to understand these chimneys as works of architecture. The architects who designed the factories did not intend to create chimneys as an aesthetic object, thus their intentions are irrelevant when considering these chimneys as art. So there is no relationship whatsoever between the artist's intentions and the consideration of a building as a work of architecture; as Goodman would say, the aesthetic functioning of a building does not depend on intentions but on the symbol system to which the building belongs. This is not to say that the chimney's final appearance is not due to their designers (or their intentions), but rather denies that these intentions cause the building's aesthetic functioning.

And third, not all works accomplish what the creator intended, i.e., there are unfulfilled and unsuccessful intentions. In these cases, intentions cannot determine a work, because they do not necessarily come through, and accordingly it makes no sense to define a work from an intentionalist perspective. In the 1996 addition to the Salk Institute in La Jolla, designed by Louis Kahn and finished in 1965, architects David Rinehart and John MacAllister intended to imitate Kahn's style. In that way, they intended to achieve homogeneity between the old and the newer parts of the complex and, ultimately, they intended to perfect Kahn's original work. Whereas the intention of taking up Kahn's style is certainly present in the work, the subsequent intention of perfecting his building is not, for the Salk Institute's new wings diminish the qualities of Kahn's building instead of exalting them. Here, then, the architects' intentions are irrelevant because they are, at least in part, unsuccessfully carried out; at best, knowing these intentions can be valuable when interpreting a building as an unsuccessful effort at transmitting them.

Intentionalism is thus rejected because intentions can be inaccessible or irrelevant to interpretation as well as to determine whether or not a building is a work of architecture. Even if there can be an interpretation based on the creator's intentions, this is only one among many other possible and valid interpretations. Similarly, despite intending to create a work of architecture, this will not make the outcome be architecture and, vice versa, despite not intending to create a work of architecture, the outcome may unintentionally be architecture. An object or a building can be interpreted in many ways, also as a work of art or architecture, precisely because it can function symbolically regardless of its creator's intentions. Or, the other way around, if works of architecture were not symbols, they would not require interpretation and their meanings and statures as architectural works would be fixed and unalterable. As Goodman affirms:

> **A work of art typically means in varied and contrasting and shifting ways and is open to many equally good and enlightening interpretations.**
>
> **(Goodman 1988: 44)**

Intentionalism is thus rejected because intentions can be inaccessible or irrelevant to interpretation as well as to determine whether or not a building is a work of architecture.

But that a work as a symbol is open to 'many equally good and enlightening interpretations' does not mean that each and every interpretation is valid. In addition to absolutism, Goodman also rejects its opposite, termed radical relativism, according to which all the interpretations of a work are valid (Goodman 1988: 44). Radical relativism is not accepted because it implies that all interpretations are extraneous to the work and that there is no criterion to determine their rightness. If each and every interpretation were valid, then the way architecture symbolically functions would be irrelevant for distinguishing between right and wrong interpretations. Architectural works are complex symbols that bear many interpretations, but it is not the case that anything goes, nor that we lack criteria to determine the adequacy of such interpretations. The Sydney Opera House can be interpreted as symbolizing a group of sails, a cluster of shells, or white messy hair, but not as symbolizing a monkey. The building itself provides a basis for our interpretations and for arguing in favour or against certain construals: the Sydney Opera's roof, formed by irregular and curved white triangles, serves to justify that the building symbolizes sails. The symbol system to which the Sydney Opera House is inserted provides the framework of interpretation, so that the shape and colour of the roof can be associated with sails.

Goodman defends instead an intermediate position between absolutism and radical relativism, termed constructive relativism (Goodman 1988: 45). Works of architecture, and in general any symbol, are open to an indeterminate number of interpretations and there are criteria to discern between right and wrong ones, such as coherency and consistency. The Jewish Museum in Berlin symbolizes the atrocities suffered by the Jewish people in the first half of the twentieth century, and it will never be an apology of anti-Semitism: the argument that the museum's shape – a decomposed Star of David – symbolizes anti-Semitism because it destroys Jewish iconography is rejected by the museum's other symbolizations and meanings (see Figure 10, p. 62). So, no matter the reasons for defending this interpretation, it is not adequate to the building nor never will be – hence, it is wrong. Construals have to be sustainable and reasonable once contrasted with the work's features as a symbol; if they are not, then they are rejected. Broadly, interpretation is a matter of fit or adequacy between interpretation and symbol within the context of a symbol system.

Goodman defends instead an intermediate position between absolutism and radical relativism, termed constructive relativism (Goodman 1988: 45).

As said, a work of architecture as an artistic symbol requires interpretation, and this entails also that it can always be misinterpreted. However, misinterpretations can be disregarded as soon as they are contrasted with the work's functioning as symbol. If I consider my apartment block as a work of architecture, this assumption is refuted once the building's symbolic functioning is examined. Affirming that the criterion of rightness of an interpretation is the symbol and its symbol system and that there can be multiple correct interpretations of the same work implies that there are no external reasons to privilege certain interpreters above others. Not only the creator's interpretation is not favoured, but the social, historical, or cultural causes that prompted certain interpretations are in themselves irrelevant for establishing the rightness of each interpretation: feminist or postcolonial interpretations of a work are not right or wrong because they are feminist or postcolonial, nor superior or inferior to others because they have a certain origin; being interpretations of a certain kind does not invalidate or validate them. Rather, some interpretations are adequate to a work and others are not, based on the work's symbolic functioning. In this way, Goodman opens the possibility of a plurality of different but equally right interpretations of a work, which are independent of the context or concerns that prompted these interpretations and also independent of arguments based on the interpreter's authority and the institutional context.

Institutionalism and Goodman's account

The central point maintained by institutional theories of art is that a work of art is conferred its status of art, or a work of architecture is conferred its status of architecture, by the so-called 'artworld'. George Dickie was the first to propose an institutional theory of art, which he later refined (Dickie 1977, 1984). Arthur Danto first developed the notion of "artworld" in 1964, although he later rejected his institutional approach and proposed another non-institutional account of art (Danto 1964, 1981; a general introduction to institutional theories of art is in Yanal 1998). Roughly, the artworld is formed by artistic institutions (such as museums, galleries, or art centres), people (such as artists, curators, art critics, or art historians), and also by a proper theoretical context as well as knowledge and understanding of art. So it is the work's institutional context that establishes what counts as an architectural work. If there are two identical objects and one is considered a work of art or architecture and the other not, this distinction is possible because the appropriate institution or member of the artworld confers the status of art or architecture to one of them and not the other.

Goodman certainly acknowledges that an object may or may not function as an artistic symbol depending on the context – in his example, a stone can function as a geological specimen in a museum of natural history, as an artwork in an art museum, and not symbolize anything at all on a road (Goodman 1978: 76; Goodman 1984: 59). But, as he says:

> I do not – as is sometimes supposed – subscribe to any 'institutional' theory of art. *Institutionalization is only one, and sometimes overemphasized and often ineffectual, means of implementation.*
>
> (Goodman 1984: 145, his emphasis)

Goodman defines implementation as a series of procedures that make 'works work' as such. That is to say, to implement means to facilitate the symbolic functioning of an object or to make something function as a symbol at all, such as happens when a stone is activated as a geological symbol in a museum of natural history or as an artwork in an art museum (Goodman 1984: 142–5). While it is true that a building can work as an architectural work depending on the context (a model house that serves to show the home's features to potential buyers is not usually a work of architecture, but it can work as such in an exhibition on housing structures), this process of implementation is neither exclusively nor necessarily undertaken by the artworld.

Institutionalization is rejected to determine what counts as architecture because it is neither necessary nor sufficient to make a work work: on the one hand, a work can function as art independently of the artworld – thus institutionalization is not necessary; on the other hand, an object can be conferred the status of art by the artworld and still not function as an artistic symbol – thus institutionalization is not sufficient. The aesthetic functioning of the house on top of the street goes unnoticed by the artworld, and yet the house still functions artistically and is hence an architectural work – institutional theories are not necessary, for the house is architecture independently from its context. It can plausibly be argued that Santiago Calatrava's umpteenth bridge, identical to several of his previous bridges, even though conferred the status of a work of art or architecture by the artworld, does not function as such – that is, institutional theories are not sufficient to make the bridge work as an artistic symbol. This example shows also that some works taken to be art or architecture will never symbolically function aesthetically no matter what the artworld undertakes. Even if one tries to make Calatrava's umpteenth bridge be a work of architecture by inserting it in an institutional context, it will probably continue failing to function as a work of architecture. The artworld is impotent in these cases.

Institutionalization is rejected to determine what counts as architecture because it is neither necessary nor sufficient to make a work work: on the one hand, a work can function as art independently of the artworld – thus institutionalization is not necessary; on the other hand, an object can be conferred the status of art by the artworld and still not function as an artistic symbol – thus institutionalization is not sufficient.

Hence Goodman's approach – according to which works of art and architecture are symbols – solves a series of problems that neither essentialist, intentionalist, nor institutional theories can overcome. First, by affirming that a building is a work of architecture only if it functions as an aesthetic symbol, Goodman provides a characterization of architecture sufficiently elastic to include past, present, and future works of architecture, and also explains how one and the same building can be both a work of architecture and simply a building that does not symbolize anything at all, or that functions as another kind of symbol. Second, by maintaining a constructive relativism according to which the rightness of several interpretations of a work depends on its symbolic functioning, Goodman provides a criterion independent of the creator's intentions. This criterion, based on the aesthetic functioning of the work, serves also to recognize misinterpretations and avoid a radical relativism. Third, by stressing that what makes a building a work of architecture is its aesthetic functioning, Goodman's account does not require any specific context, i.e., the artworld, which would confer on the work its artistic status.

interpretation is not extraneous to the work but constitutive of the work itself

As mentioned earlier, Goodman's way to solve the problems other approaches entail is a functionalist, pluralist, pragmatic, and constructivist account of art and architecture. It is a functionalist and pluralist approach, for the same object can function in many different ways depending on the symbolic context; it implies also that everything is able to be aesthetically perceived and that, given the proper symbol system, any building could potentially be architecture. Goodman's account is also a pragmatic or, in linguistic terms, a performative one, because his analysis focuses on the active and functional aspects of art: he is concerned with how works work, function, or operate as symbols and how in this way they convey meaning. His aim is not to find out and discuss the origin and causes of symbolic functioning; ontological aspects of art and architecture are set aside, precisely because Goodman maintains that no progress has been made by asking such essentialist questions. In this pragmatic context, interpretation plays a central role, because through interpretation we distinguish what functions as architecture or as another sort of symbol, and we also determine what and how a building means. That is to say, interpretation of a symbol's meaning goes hand by hand with determining what kind of symbol something is. Even more, interpretation is not extraneous to the work but constitutive of the work itself, which is why Goodman's account is a constructivist one:

> More than any other art, architecture makes us aware that interpretation cannot be so easily distinguished from the work. A painting can be presented all at once ... but a building has to be put together from a heterogeneous assortment of visual and kinesthetic experiences: from views at different distances and angles, from walks through the interior, from climbing stairs and straining necks, from photographs, miniature models, sketches, plans, and from actual use. Such construction of the work as known is itself of the same sort as interpretation and will be affected by our ideas about the building and by what it and its parts mean or are coming to mean. ... Stripping off or ripping out all construals (that is, all interpretation and construction) does not leave a work cleansed of all encrustation but demolishes it.
>
> (Goodman 1988: 44–5)

Two important aspects are discussed in this excerpt: first, that interpretation is as constitutive of a building as are its material elements. The idea that 'stripping off or ripping out all construals … demolishes' a building is meant in a strong sense. Plainly, as if it were an onion, taking out all the interpretative layers that constitute a work does not lead to its core, but leaves us with nothing. It is in this strong sense that what a symbol means is also what constitutes a world or world-version, and architects, inasmuch as they design and create buildings, are also fundamentally symbol-makers and world-makers: compelling buildings are open to many enriching interpretations, they foster the creation of meaning and understanding and thus the construction of significant world-versions (as is discussed in the last chapter). Goodman's constructive relativism, according to which there are multiple and equally right interpretations of a work, has its ontological counterpart, so that there are multiple and equally right versions of the world. The criteria to evaluate the rightness of an interpretation are also the ones to assess the rightness of a world-version. The process of interpreting an architectural work, and also of constructing it, happens when aesthetically perceiving and experiencing a work, which is the second important issue mentioned in the quotation above that needs to be examined.

architects, inasmuch as they design and create buildings, are also fundamentally symbol-makers and world-makers

Aesthetic experience of architecture

Several authors have commented on aesthetic experience of architecture from various philosophical perspectives (see, for instance, Rasmussen 1959; Scruton 1979; Mitias 1999; Carlson 2000; Rush 2009). For Goodman, aesthetic attitude is not a passive state of contemplation in which a work is perceived in a state of purity, but an active engagement where a series of experiences and previous knowledge are put together and a work is interpreted as an artistic symbol:

> **The aesthetic 'attitude' is restless, searching, testing – is less attitude than action: creation and re-creation.**
>
> **(Goodman 1968: 242)**

So aesthetic experience is mainly a cognitive endeavour, a 'dynamic' process that 'involves making delicate discriminations and discerning subtle relationships' (Goodman 1968: 241); it is an interpretative process where the work's meanings come to light. Within this cognitive and active framework, aesthetic experience of architecture presents some particularities that are mainly given by the specific features of buildings and other constructions and that distinguish it from the aesthetic experience of the other arts.

Aesthetic experience of architecture usually begins with the perception of the work, although our initial contact with a building can also be through a plan, image, or description. While in the other arts there is generally a sense that prevails over the others (sight in visual arts, hearing in music), a building is experienced and perceived with all the senses interacting with each other. Perception of architecture is multisensory: through vision, form and space are perceived; through hearing, the building's acoustic features; through touch, smell and even taste, temperature, humidity and qualities of the constructing materials are experienced. Even more, perception is a bodily experience, in the sense that when appreciating a building we interact with our entire body: we walk through and establish a spatial relation with the work; we hear the echo of our steps, the creaking of the materials; we perceive the warmth of sunshine or the cold in air-conditioned rooms; we smell the wood of floors and panels or freshly painted walls. Our experience is also bodily in that our senses are conditioned by our body and movements. To see something we turn our head and our perspective is constantly changing when moving, sitting, looking up or down, and more generally, our perception depends on our actual size, the speed at which we move, on our particular physical features.

Perception of the work is also determined by the difference in size between building and person:

> [A]n architectural work contrasts with other works of art in scale. A building or park or city is not only bigger spatially and temporally than a musical performance or painting, it is bigger even than we are. We cannot

**take it all in from a single point of view; we must move around and within
it to grasp the whole.**

(Goodman 1988: 32)

While paintings are experienced as hanging in front of us and we can decide
whether or not to contemplate them, buildings impose themselves on the
appreciator and it is quite difficult to ignore them. We can perceive a building
as surrounding us or, the other way around, we perceive the building by
surrounding it. An architectural work can hence not be experienced at once,
but perceiving interior and exterior, front, back and lateral façades, the
several floors if any, is necessarily a temporal and sequential experience. Our
perceptions are unified, creating a whole that we have actually never perceived;
as already quoted, a 'building has to be put together from a heterogeneous
assortment of … experiences' (Goodman 1988: 45). Thus, perception is already
a construction; there is no pure perception but a cognitive construction created
from our previous fragmented perceptions. And this perception is cognitive,
as is clear if one considers that it is already influenced, as Goodman states,
by our previous knowledge and experiences. The perception of a building
may be shaped by specific knowledge provided by plans, models, projections,
drawings, photographs, aerial views, or virtual walks, given that these can
help us in orienting ourselves in the building and in recognizing parts and
elements *in situ*. Our prior conceptions and knowledge of all kinds is helpful
in distinguishing features or details; knowing about architectural styles helps
us in recognizing an arch as Romanesque or Gothic and in that way guide our
perception of the building. Previous experiences of other works can also shape
the subsequent perception of other buildings: if we have in mind the spatial
experience of one of the Romanesque churches at the Vall de Boí when visiting
the Cathedral of Barcelona, we will probably experience the Cathedral's inner
space as light and vast. But if we compare this perception of the Cathedral's
nave with the one of the nearby Gothic church of Santa Maria del Mar, then
we will probably perceive the Cathedral as much heavier and massive than
when having a Romanesque church in mind.

perception is already a construction

Another aspect that distinguishes architecture from most of the other arts and that shapes our aesthetic experience is the site or location of a building:

> Unlike a painting that may be reframed or rehung or a concerto that may be heard in different halls, the architectural work is firmly set in a physical and cultural environment that alters slowly.
>
> (Goodman 1988: 32)

Whereas paintings and musical pieces are usually not site-specific, architecture is generally site-specific. Apart from mobile homes, tents, and other transportable structures, buildings are bound to a site – a physical and cultural site in constant change. The building's site may influence our aesthetic experience and hence its surroundings should be taken into account. By comparing a certain building with the adjacent buildings, size relations are established: one can realize whether it is proportioned in relation the other ones or whether it fits on the place it is built. In some cases, site becomes a constitutive element of the building, as in Frank Lloyd Wright's Fallingwater House. While in other arts it is usually not necessary to consider the physical

Figure 1 Corinthian columns of the Temple of Augustus in Barcelona.

location of a work (with the exception of certain sculptures, installations, and land art), in architecture it is required to appreciate the work in its entirety.

In addition to site, there are other aspects related to the building's location that may influence our aesthetic appreciation. While the height at which a painting hangs on the wall or the exact position of a sculpture in a gallery is generally irrelevant when aesthetically appreciating a work (as long as the works are not so inconveniently displayed that our perception is obstructed), the building's orientation and placement within the site must indeed be considered. Obviously, works of art may occupy a specific position in an exhibition due to a curatorial discourse, and then the work's placement creates a relationship among works that is certainly relevant. The same may happen with architectural works when their plans and models are displayed in a way that makes them interact with each other. So, not only the physical but also the cultural environment may play a role in our appreciation of a building, for some aspects may be pointed out and others minimized depending on their cultural context. The four remaining Corinthian columns of the Temple of Augustus in Barcelona are not surrounded by other Roman relics, but inside the patio of a Gothic house (Figure 1). They are not perceived as part of a temple in the middle of the old Roman Barcino, inside the Forum and on the top of Mount Taber, but rather as a structural part of the later house placed just behind the cathedral, providing us with an insight into how Roman remains were appreciated in medieval times. These columns were rediscovered at the end of the nineteenth century, when they were again appreciated as artistic artefacts, and therefore isolated from the building's structure and shown to the public. Now they are displayed in such a way that one is able to understand the changes in perception and interpretation of the columns throughout history. Thus the cultural environment influences our appreciation of the columns in a way that enhances and alters both our appreciation and, as Goodman emphasizes, their meaning.

Compared to the other arts, architecture is eminently public. Buildings impose themselves in the space where most of the population lives and this entails that it cannot be ignored: whereas we can decide not to enter a museum to see the artworks it hosts, we cannot close our eyes to our vital environment. Architecture is part of the public sphere, and as such it may have an ethical and political role. In addition to this, buildings are objects that are collectively perceived and used in our everyday life, which entails that the buildings' practical function can prevail over their aesthetic function; this is precisely the concern of everyday aesthetics (Light and Smith 2005; Saito 2007; Bhatt 2013). This is another aspect that distinguishes our experience of architecture from the experience of other arts, for we occupy and use buildings for many purposes that usually have nothing to do with aesthetics. To perceive a building aesthetically requires a detachment from its practical function, even though this practical function can influence its aesthetic functioning. As Goodman says:

> [I]n architecture as in few other arts, a work usually has a practical function, such as protecting and facilitating certain activities, that is no less important than, and often dominates, its aesthetic function.
>
> (Goodman 1988: 32)

People working in the Seagram Building in New York may only perceive this skyscraper as their office space and pay attention to the practical features that influence their work: they know whether the heating system is too strong in winter and the air conditioning too weak in summer, know which elevator is faster, and complain that the window blinds have only three positions – fully open, halfway open, and fully closed – which makes it quite difficult to control the amount of natural light in the office room. Only by detaching themselves from their everyday experience of the Seagram Building are they able to aesthetically appreciate it: the building's structural elements are articulated and a glass and steel curtain wall with no structural function is hung on them; the window blinds' three positions, so annoying when working, are now understood as a way to achieve a regular pattern in the façade and avoid a disorganized appearance because of the employees drawing the blinds to different heights. The building's practical function may influence its aesthetic function and, vice versa, its aesthetic function may influence the practical one. The possibility of distinguishing our everyday experience from the aesthetic experience is what enables one and the same building to be considered as both a work of art and simply as a building.

Hence, aesthetic experience of architecture is a dynamic process determined by the building's specific features, such as size, functionality, and location, and by the fact that, unlike most of the other arts, in architecture all the five senses are involved in perception. Despite Goodman's emphasis that aesthetic experience is primarily a cognitive engagement, this does not mean that it cannot be pleasurable or that it does not involve feelings and emotions. Rather, since not all artworks produce pleasure or awaken emotions (as happens with some conceptual artworks), pleasure and emotion are not criteria to establish what functions as a work of art or architecture. For Goodman, the main purpose of architecture and art is to foster understanding (and to further create world-versions) and, in this conceptual framework, feelings and emotions are already cognitive:

> [I]n aesthetic experience the *emotions function cognitively*. The work of art is apprehended through the feelings as well as through the senses.
>
> (Goodman 1968: 248, his emphasis)

When aesthetically experiencing a work, emotions and feelings, like our senses, serve to discern the work's symbolic functioning. Whereas through the senses we perceive certain qualities of a building, the feeling awakened by it – the experience of looking up to a skyscraper from one of its corners or the oppression felt in a small crypt – can help us in distinguishing the features of a certain building that otherwise would not be experienced. These emotions do not function independently from the rest of our cognitive and sensorial faculties, but are one element among the many others engaged in aesthetic experience. That is to say, in art,

> emotion and cognition are interdependent: feeling without understanding is blind, and understanding without feeling is empty.
>
> (Goodman 1984: 8)

If we could not retain what we feel when entering a small and dark crypt, this emotion would be useless; with no emotion, there is nothing to retain. This does not mean, however, that emotions are being intellectualized, but rather that cognition is being sensitized: both are inextricably linked and need each other in aesthetic experience as well as in understanding in general.

Hence, aesthetic experience of architecture is a dynamic process determined by the building's specific features, such as size, functionality, and location, and by the fact that, unlike most of the other arts, in architecture all the five senses are involved in perception.

So, asking 'When is architecture?' rather than 'What is architecture?' implies placing architecture in a completely different context and opens the philosophical investigation towards a new and fruitful area. By stating that a building is architecture when it functions as an aesthetic symbol, not only the difficulties that essentialist, intentionalist, and institutionalist accounts present are overcome, but architecture acquires a fundamental role in the construction of meaning and reality. Goodman's pluralist and functional approach thus entails that a building can function as a symbol that conveys several meanings in various ways. As a symbol, it is open to multiple interpretations (and misinterpretations), and by means of criteria such as coherency and consistency with the features of both symbol and symbol system we can distinguish between right and wrong ones. Through aesthetic experience, understood not as passive contemplation but as an active endeavour, we unfold the work's meanings and interpret them. Features such as the size, location, and practical function of buildings determine our aesthetic experience of architecture and also the building's meanings and interpretations. These various construals of the work are not extraneous to, but rather constitutive of, the work itself. This entails that while aesthetically experiencing an architectural work we are also construing and constructing a world. Likewise, architects do not simply make things by 'molding mud' (Goodman 1984: 42), but inasmuch as their creations are symbols, they are both symbol-makers as well as world-makers.

architects do not simply make things by 'molding mud'

CHAPTER 3

Buildings as Symbols

The vocabulary of reference and related terms is vast: within a few brief passages from a couple of essays on architecture, we may read of buildings that allude, express, evoke, invoke, comment, quote; that are syntactical, literal, metaphorical, dialectical; that are ambiguous or even contradictory! All these terms and many more have to do in one way or another with reference and may help us to grasp what a building means.

(Goodman 1988: 33–4)

To say that buildings refer is to say that buildings are symbols; it entails that in addition to providing shelter or fulfilling any other practical function, they also convey meanings. It is necessary then to examine what it means that buildings and other architectural structures function as symbols and in that way categorize and make sense of concepts such as allusion, evocation, quotation, metaphor, or even contradiction in architecture. This chapter thus describes Goodman's notions of symbol and symbol system, comments on the several ways of referring, and on how to detect and evaluate these symbolizations. It focuses on the particularities of symbolization in architecture to better understand how architects may contribute to the advancement of understanding and to the further making and remaking of worlds or world-versions.

Symbol and symbol systems

Goodman uses 'symbol' as a 'very general and colorless term' (Goodman 1968: xi): something is a symbol of something if it refers to it. 'Reference' is also used in a very general sense, including 'all cases of *standing for*' (Goodman 1984: 55). This primitive relation constitutes the keystone of the theory and as such cannot be defined by any external notion, but is rather elucidated by the different modes in which reference takes place. If it were possible to define 'reference', it would mean having to resort to notions external to the system and, by doing so, those notions would be introduced to the system so that 'reference' would no longer be a primitive term. It is not possible either to resort to internal notions to define a primitive term, because then one would fall into a circular argument. That is the reason why primitive or basic notions are explicated and not defined, as Aristotle already argued (*Posterior Analytics* II, 19 in Aristotle 1993: 72–4; see also Goodman 1984: 55; Goodman 1988: 124; Vermaulen *et al.* 2009). Reference is thus explicated through its two main modes – denotation and exemplification, and also through expression and the various modes of complex and indirect reference, such as allusion, variation, and style. The modes of reference are how a symbol means; what a symbol means is determined by the symbol system.

Symbols do not stand alone, but are part of a system composed of a scheme and a field of reference or realm. There are several kinds of symbol systems (such as notational, verbal, musical, and pictorial), with semantic and syntactic features that determine the symbols' meanings and how we interpret them. A symbol scheme is compounded by a collection of characters with rules to combine them. Each character is compounded by marks and the rules of the scheme determine also what marks correspond to what character. The scheme of a symbol system such as the English language is made of the letters of the Latin alphabet as well as of syntactic rules that determine, for example, that 'a' and 'A' are marks of the same character and that 'hut' is a compound character of the scheme but 'htu' is not. The symbol system is regulated also by semantic rules, which determine the field of reference and specify, for instance, that 'hut' refers to a certain kind of dwelling and not to something to cover one's head, as is the case of 'hut' in the symbol system of the German language.

The modes of reference are how a symbol means; what a symbol means is determined by the symbol system.

The several kinds of symbol systems differ among each other because of their semantic and syntactic features. Depending on whether these features are more or less strict, one can classify the kinds of systems in a continuum that ranges from differentiated or attenuated to non-differentiated or dense systems. Notations are systems that fulfil the strictest conditions and can be placed at the differentiated end of the variety of symbol systems (Goodman 1968: 127–73; Elgin 1983: 104–13). In a notation, one symbol of the scheme has only one referent in the realm and each referent corresponds only to one symbol in the scheme; taking Elgin's example, this happens with the postcode system, where a single code corresponds to only one area and each area has only one code. Syntactically, notations are character-indifferent, for the several marks of a character are interchangeable: 10025, *10025*, and **10025** refer all to the same postcode area; they are syntactically disjoint, for each mark belongs to no more than one character: 1, *1*, and **1** belong to only the character one of the Arabic numeral system; and they are finitely differentiated, for in theory it is always possible to establish to which character a mark belongs (sometimes 1 can be mistaken by the lower case letter l, hence this aspect of notations is only valid in theory and not in practice). Semantically, notations are unambiguous, for the characters have only one referent or compliance class: 10025 corresponds to a single geographical area in New York City; they are disjoint, for the several referents or compliance classes do not intersect among each other: the postcode areas are not superimposed; and they are finitely differentiated, for it is always possible to establish to which symbol an object of the field of reference corresponds: given an area, we can determine its postcode univocally.

Other symbol systems have notational features but are not as perfect: the Western musical notation fulfils most of the requirements to being a notation, but not the requirement of semantic disjointness, because the same sound can correspond to more than one character – the same pitch corresponds to C-sharp and D-flat, for instance. Natural languages are notational schemes rather than notational systems, because they fulfil the syntactic but not the semantic requirements: English contains ambiguous terms (such as 'right' and 'cape') and is semantically non-disjoint ('building' and 'hut' share some referents). Plans, elevations, and sections constitute the notations for architecture. Roughly, they are codified drawings usually at scale that refer to elements of a construction (existing or to be built). In a floor plan, a circle denotes a column, two lines denote a new wall, two lines with poché denote an existing wall, a thin line with an arch, a door and its opening direction, and so on. This symbolization is usually accompanied by numbers, symbols that indicate the exact measurements of each element, and sometimes also by written specifications, i.e., other sorts of symbols that may indicate functions or materials (such as 'bedroom' or 'glass'). Notations in architecture include several ways of reference that, taken together, create complex symbols. In addition to their practical function of helping out in the construction process, for Goodman, plans, elevations, and sections have another, very specific function, which is that of fixing the identity of a certain sort of works of art and architecture, termed allographic. Chapter 4 explains the role of notations in determining identity and examines closer the characteristics of architecture's notations determining whether they are notational systems or notational schemes, that is, whether they resemble more the notation for music – scores, or the notation for drama – scripts.

Plans, elevations, and sections constitute the notations for architecture.

Finally, other systems are not notational at all, for none of the syntactic and semantic requirements of notations are fulfilled. Such is the case of pictorial systems, which in Goodman's terms are syntactically and semantically dense. Dense systems are syntactically and semantically non-disjoint, which means that there is no way to tell to what character a mark corresponds, nor to what exact element the symbol refers to and, in addition, any minute difference in the system's components makes a relevant difference to symbolization. Take, for example, an architectural sketch of a Bathing Pavilion by RCR Arquitectes in Olot, Spain (Figure 2). There is no way to determine what constitutes a mark or a character (one cannot tell whether the several tonalities of grey are marks or characters, nor it is possible to delimit them), nor to assign any particular referent to any element of the sketch (there is no way to tell whether the brushstroke representing the river also represents the different tonalities of the water, the stream alone, or the stream together with the riverbed). Pictorial systems are also relatively replete, which is a feature that differentiates them from other representational systems such as diagrams. Consider Goodman's example comparing an electrocardiogram with a Hokusai drawing of Mount Fujiyama (Goodman 1968: 229). Both look the same: an undulating black line on a white background. The difference lies in that the drawing symbolizes along more dimensions than the electrocardiogram: whereas thickness and colour of the line are irrelevant

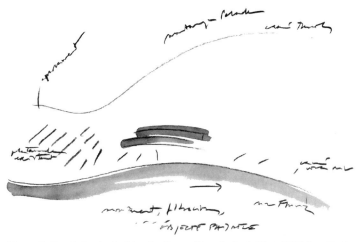

Figure 2 Sketch for the Bathing Pavilion at Tussols-Basil, Olot. RCR Arquitectes.

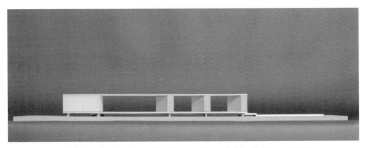

Figure 3 Model for the Bathing Pavilion at Tussols-Basil, Olot. RCR Arquitectes.

in the electrocardiogram, they are an essential feature of the drawing. Both painting and diagram are not articulated, but the first is relatively replete and the second is attenuated. The same difference is found, for example, between an initial sketch (Figure 2) and an architectural model of the Bathing Pavilion (Figure 3). The sketch is relatively replete because all of its elements are relevant to its symbolic functioning. On the other hand, the model – a three-dimensional diagram that represents a structure at scale – is attenuated because only certain elements matter: it symbolizes volumes and proportions, but not the materials (concrete and corten steel); and even though shadows are present in the model, they do not stand for the exact shadows cast on the building. The model is thus attenuated. The difference between these two does not depend on the fact that sketches are two-dimensional and models three-dimensional, but rather on the symbol system. There are initial models that symbolize similarly to the discussed sketch – they are more replete, and there are renderings that symbolize similarly to the abovementioned model – they are more attenuated. Photographs and the finished structure have yet other features: they are replete and dense throughout (Figure 4).

Figure 4 Bathing Pavilion at Tussols-Basil, Olot. RCR Arquitectes.

in architecture the whole range of systems is present: plans, elevations, sections, models, diagrams, drawings, renderings, sketches, and buildings themselves, can be placed in the continuum constituted by the kinds of symbol systems.

Symbol systems, then, extend from attenuated to dense, from notations to pictorial systems, and in architecture the whole range of systems is present: plans, elevations, sections, models, diagrams, drawings, renderings, sketches, and buildings themselves, all of them – as symbols within systems – can be placed in the continuum constituted by the kinds of symbol systems. There is not always a clear separation between them and sometimes several symbol systems coexist, as happens in floor plans that include drawing at scale, numbers, and linguistic instructions. These three symbol systems share notational features, but this does not need to be so; there are mixed cases that contain dense and attenuated elements:

> **A scale model of a campus, with green papier-mâché for grass, pink cardboard for brick, plastic film for glass, etc., is analog with respect to spatial dimensions but digital with respect to materials.**
>
> **(Goodman 1968: 173)**

The distinction between analogue and digital systems is another way to describe the difference between dense and non-dense. The model described in this last passage symbolizes dimensions analogically, because no exact measures are given nor can be extrapolated from the model – it is dense throughout. Materials, on the contrary, are symbolized digitally, because each material in the model refers to only one construction material and each construction material is only referred to by one material in the model. The difference between analogue and digital systems (dense and non-dense) is exemplified by the different symbolic functioning between analogue and digital thermometers: whereas in a digital thermometer a determinate temperature is given, in an analogue thermometer there is no way to tell the exact measurement the mercury indicates (Goodman 1968: 159–64). Architectural sketches and drawings would then be analogue and can be placed at the other end of the spectrum of symbol systems, opposite from notations.

Buildings, and symbols of any kind, function within one or more symbol systems and therefore can have several referents and symbolize in various ways. One needs to know about – or at least be minimally familiar with – the symbol system in order to interpret the symbol properly. A church symbolizes Christianity, a mosque Islam, and a synagogue Judaism in a system similar to the notational ones that relates architectural typologies with religions. But the same church symbolizes the Gothic in a system that relates buildings to styles, and further refers to a certain mood, grandiosity, or the sacred in a dense system with features similar to the pictorial ones, where every difference makes a difference to the work's symbolic functioning. Certain knowledge – or at least a rough understanding – about kinds of religions and sacred buildings is needed to interpret those buildings as referring to a particular belief, and about architectural styles to interpret a church as referring to the Gothic. Obviously, the more one knows, the abler one is to interpret the building's meanings. Both the French and the Norman Gothic windows have two arches set within them, but only those who know their particular characteristics can determine whether a church symbolizes one or the other. Within symbol systems, buildings refer in different modes.

Denotation

Denotation is the relation between a label and what it labels. These labels are not only verbal: the word 'house' and its utterance, a description, a picture and a model of a house, all of them denote a house. There are symbols that denote a single object ('Taj Mahal'), others that denote generally ('building'), and others that do not denote anything or have null denotation ('Tower of Babel'). In this last case, the meaning is determined by the group of descriptions and depictions of the Tower of Babel and these are what distinguish symbols with null reference from one another: both 'Tower of

Babel' and 'Hogwarts Castle' have null denotation, but they are not the same symbol because their descriptions and depictions differ. In Goodman's technical terms, symbols with null denotation share a primary extension (nothing) but differ in their secondary extensions (the several descriptions and depictions). Thus when lacking a referent, the label does not denote its primary extension, but is denoted by its several secondary extensions (Goodman 1984: 77–80).

Even though buildings do not usually denote, there are plans, elevations, and sections that notationally denote; the relatively few cases of verbal and pictorial denotation as well as of quotation are worth examining to better understand how copies, reproductions, and fictional buildings symbolize.

Denotation can be literal and metaphorical: 'green building' denotes a building painted green as well as an environmentally friendly building. Goodman lists four kinds of denotation: verbal, pictorial, quotation, and notation (Goodman 1984: 55–9). Even though buildings do not usually denote, there are plans, elevations, and sections that notationally denote; the relatively few cases of verbal and pictorial denotation as well as of quotation are worth examining to better understand how reproductions, and fictional buildings symbolize.

Verbal denotation in architecture is found, first of all, in inscriptions, inasmuch as they are taken to be parts of the building and not superimposed elements. It also occurs when some part or an entire building can be considered as functioning within a verbal system, i.e., when, due to their shapes, they can be interpreted as letters. So the beams at the Modern Art Museum of Fort Worth, Texas may be taken to symbolize the letter 'y' and the headquarters of the Gas Natural company in Barcelona symbolize a capital 'l'. The context may help in disambiguating some cases: the circular-shape structure at the Graduate House of the University of Toronto refers to the vowel 'o' and not the number zero, as it conforms the last letter of the word 'Toronto', half-printed, half-shaped on the building's façade.

Pictorial denotation in architecture occurs when buildings symbolize like paintings that represent something. As with verbal denotation, there are some elements of buildings, such as mosaics, sculptures, and reliefs, that represent, but can only be considered as examples of pictorial denotation in architecture if taken as constitutive and not superimposed parts of the building. Proper architectural cases of pictoral denotation would be the towers of Antoni Gaudí's Sagrada Família representing the nearby mountain of Montserrat (Goodman 1988: 34, 37), the Sydney Opera House representing sails, shells, or white messy hair, the Dunmore Pavilion in Scotland representing a pineapple (see Figure 9, p. 60), and buildings shaped like donuts, milk bottles, ice creams, or clam boxes representing the products sold there.

A particular case of buildings representing in their entirety is that of copies or reproductions. The several reproductions of the Eiffel Tower throughout the world among others, one in Las Vegas, one in Paris (Texas), another in Paris (Tennessee), and two in China represent the Eiffel Tower in Paris, France. The Parthenon in Nashville (Tennessee) is a copy of – and hence represents – the Parthenon in Athens. That copies represent other buildings does not necessarily entail that they also symbolize the same as the original. What differentiates the building represented from the building that represents is that the second one refers to the first one, whereas the first one does not represent the second one nor, generally, itself. The Eiffel Tower in Las Vegas represents the one in Paris (France), but the one in France does not represent the one in Las Vegas nor does it represent itself; the tower in Las Vegas does not represent the one in Texas, either. Copies thus have a symbolic function – that of representing another building – that the buildings they are copies of lack. Apart from that, a reproduction may or may not symbolize the same as the building represented and, if it symbolizes the same, it does not need to symbolize in the same way. Both the Eiffel Tower in Paris and the one in Las Vegas symbolize France, but the one in Paris also symbolizes the centennial of the French Revolution (it was dedicated in 1889) and French technological power at the end of the nineteenth century. The Eiffel Tower in Las Vegas may symbolize the centennial of the French Revolution via a chain of reference. But it would be more difficult to maintain that it symbolizes French technological power at the end of the nineteenth century, for the Eiffel Tower in Las Vegas was built in 1999 with contemporary techniques and, therefore, the properties of being built in 1889 and of being a highlight of French technological power that the Eiffel Tower in Paris, France, symbolizes are not present in the reproduction. Other symbolizations of the original may also get lost in the copy: that the reproduction in Las Vegas is half-scale to the original entails that all that which the Eiffel Tower symbolizes because of its size, such as grandeur, is not symbolized by its reproduction, unless one considers that the Eiffel Tower in Las Vegas symbolizes grandeur ironically. Closely related to the issue of copies and reproductions is that of identity: while the Parthenon in Nashville is a copy of the one in Athens, the several identical houses in a tract housing neighbourhood are not considered copies, but rather instances of the same work. This differentiation is examined in the next chapter.

Contrary to what one may assume, representation does not require resemblance to the object denoted. First, while resemblance is symmetric, representation is not, for what most resembles an object is the object itself, but an object usually does not represent itself; and while resemblance is reciprocal, representation is not: the Dunmore Pavilion represents a pineapple, but a pineapple does not represent the Dunmore Pavilion. Second, there is no way to privilege one sort of resemblance over others, so that this could allow us to establish the most adequate resemblance criteria for representation. A photo of the Sagrada Família, its negative, Gaudí's drawings, a souvenir, a virtual model, and any other depiction represent and resemble the Sagrada Família; they do not represent it in the same way, but all of them are equally valid representations. Third, representation is not based on imitation or copying, for it is not clear what features under what circumstances are to be imitated to represent an object and even imperfect copies may represent: a painting depicting only the four pinnacles of the Sagrada Família may still represent the entire church, as may an unfinished drawing.

Contrary to what one may assume, representation does not require resemblance to the object denoted.

There are cases that clearly show that representation is not based on resemblance to reality. As with verbal denotation, pictorial denotation may refer in multiple and general ways: TWA's terminal at New York's JFK Airport represents a bird with its wings spread and ready to take off, but it does not represent any bird in particular that actually exists, hence resemblance to reality is not an issue for representation. Pictorial denotation may also not refer to anything or have null denotation, such as Juliet's House in Verona and the Cinderella and Sleeping Beauty Castles in the Disney resorts. This is the reason why Goodman differentiates between 'picture of' and 'x-picture': in a 'picture of' what is depicted exists and in an 'x-picture' it may exist or not. In other words, 'picture of' is a category within that of 'x-picture': from all the paintings representing houses, only some represent existing houses; from all house-pictures only the ones that represent existing houses are pictures of houses (Goodman 1968: 21–6). Juliet's House is thus a 'Juliet's House-representation', that is, a symbol and not that which is referred to in *Romeo and Juliet*. This case is certainly confusing, for it is the only built representation of the Capulets' residency, it is located in the same city where Shakespeare's drama takes place and, for tourism purposes, it falsely claims to be one of the actual settings of the drama, so that it seems as if the house described by Shakespeare would be a 'description of' a real existing house in Verona, which would be the one we can now visit. While confusions generally do not arise with paintings and sculptures fictionally representing, buildings with null or fictive reference may be taken as being that which is denoted and not that which denotes, for they function in a realistic system and with a realistic symbolization: buildings fictionally representing are three-dimensional, have the same size as an actual building, and are built with actual construction materials, just as are buildings that do not represent anything. Moreover, buildings not denoting anything may nevertheless symbolize other things in other ways and perform a practical function, which may obscure their symbolic fictional character. Juliet's House functions extremely well as a tourist attraction; it perfectly fulfils the basic practical function of sheltering an activity, and it may also symbolize a place for eternal love or the way houses were restored in the mid-twentieth century.

In addition to differentiating between 'x-pictures' and 'pictures of', Goodman proposes another distinction to further understand pictorial denotation, which is the one between 'representation' and 'representation-as' (Goodman 1968: 27–31). Typical cases of representation-as are caricatures representing someone as someone or something else; an example for representation-as would be the Sleeping Beauty Castle at Disneyland, which represents this fairy-tale castle as Neuschwanstein Castle, the palace of Ludwig II of Bavaria. The difference between representation and representation-as has nothing to do with resemblance, but rather with classification: all the paintings and descriptions denoting as Neuschwanstein Castle constitute a subgroup of denoting symbols. This organization may emphasize some common elements, point out features previously unnoticed, and distinguish this representation-as from others. Depicting the Sleeping Beauty Castle as Neuschwanstein Castle may bring one to link the fairy tale with the fantasy world in which Ludwig II (also known as the *Märchenkönig* or Fairy Tale King) lived, and bring about a series of symbolizations that another Sleeping Beauty Castle-denotation (such as the description found in the story by the Grimm Brothers) does not; representation-as has thus a relevant cognitive role (Elgin 2010). So, both verbal and pictorial denotation are means of classifying rather than representing reality; how they contribute to the process of worldmaking is discussed in the last chapter.

Finally, quotation is a kind of denotation found mainly in verbal systems whose particularity is that it requires containment and reference, i.e., 'what is quoted must be included within the quoting symbol' (Goodman 1984: 58; see also Goodman 1978: 41–56). This last sentence contains a fragment and refers to it, hence it quotes. There are two sorts of quotation: direct quotation – indicated through quotation marks, and indirect quotation – indicated with an expression such as 'they said that…' or alike. In this last case, that which is quoted can be replicated or paraphrased. By analogy, for a building to quote it has to both contain and refer to what is being quoted. However, quotation in architecture is more complex than verbal quotation, mainly in that it is not just a kind of denotation but requires also exemplification. Although sometimes buildings contain other buildings (the Stalin Museum in Gori contains Stalin's birth house), a building cannot be put into quotation marks in order to quote it. In addition, it is problematic to establish what would constitute a proper replica of a building such that it could be quoted within another building (Stalin's birth house is the actual birth house, not a replica, thus the Museum cannot quote it because there is no other original house to quote from). However, it can still be said that buildings quote if both the containment and the reference requirement are taken in a broader sense, so that there is no need that a building exactly contain that which is quoted nor that only devices such as quotation marks or indirect expressions are needed to establish reference. Construed this way, it can be understood that the symbolic relation of Bernard Tschumi's Lerner Hall at Columbia University and of Aldo Rossi's apartment buildings in Perugia and Berlin to Filarete's Ca' del Duca Palace in Venice is that of quotation (Figures 5, 6 and 7), because Tschumi's and Rossi's buildings contain a column without capital at the corner which are precisely a reference by quotation to Filarete's column at the corner of that palace (see Capdevila-Werning 2011).

Figure 5 Lerner Hall at Columbia University. Bernard Tschumi.

Figure 6 Apartments at Wilhelmstrasse in Berlin. Aldo Rossi.

Figure 7 Filarete's Column at Ca' del Duca, Venice.

Exemplification

The second main mode of reference is exemplification, 'one of the major ways that architectural works mean' (Goodman 1988: 36). Goodman characterizes exemplification as 'possession plus reference' (Goodman 1968: 53); a symbol exemplifies when it both has and refers to some of its actually possessed properties, but not all of them. Exemplification is selective. A tailor's swatch possesses an indefinite amount of properties, but only exemplifies some of them: it generally exemplifies texture, colour, and pattern, but not size, shape, nor when and where it was made (Goodman 1978: 63–5). Similarly, a model house generally exemplifies size and number of rooms, distribution, and construction materials, but not its location, accessories, furniture, wall colours, nor that it was built by a certain company.

While denotation only implies a relation from the label to that which is labelled (from the label 'red' to a red paint sample), exemplification entails a double relation: from that which is labelled to the label and from the label back to the labelled (from the red sample to the label 'red' and back to the red sample, where the paint sample is actually red, i.e., has the property of being red). What a symbol exemplifies cannot always be accurately verbalized: there is no word for a red's exact tonality, glossiness, or reaction to light, but this does not mean that the referent is lacking. Rather, precisely because sometimes there is no exact verbal equivalent to the exemplified properties, we resort to an example or sample, as happens when we choose a paint colour. Exemplification provides a privileged epistemic access to certain properties that otherwise would remain obscure. A model house exemplifies features, such as the building's materials, that are certainly also denoted by the blue prints, but by exemplifying certain particularities of these materials a unique understanding is gained.

Exemplification provides a privileged epistemic access to certain properties that otherwise would remain obscure.

46   BUILDINGS AS SYMBOLS

> Works of architecture and art are a very special kind of sample, they are 'samples from the sea' (Goodman 1978: 137). This means that we never know what we will find and that, unlike a paint sample, whose interpretation is straightforward, the interpretation of a work of architecture is open-ended and never-ending.

Exemplification is present in most of our practices: samples, examples, and exemplars come into play when visiting a model house, choosing the wall colour, learning a mathematical theorem, tuning an orchestra, performing a scientific experiment, or conjugating a verb. Exemplification is also present in the arts. As with any other symbol, what is exemplified is determined by the symbol system and interpretation is required to figure out the symbol's meanings. But whereas samples and examples usually function in well-established and fixed systems, works of architecture and art do not – they are inserted in dense systems. While paint samples are commonly interpreted in one way, works of architecture and art are open to multiple and equally correct interpretations. And whereas samples usually symbolize only certain properties (colour and finish) in one way (through exemplification), works of art and architecture may symbolize several features in multiple ways. Exemplification in the arts is nevertheless selective: despite possessing them, a work does not usually exemplify its weight or the date it was finished. Works of architecture and art are a very special kind of sample, they are 'samples from the sea' (Goodman 1978: 137). This means that we never know what we will find and that, unlike a paint sample, whose interpretation is straightforward, the interpretation of a work of architecture is open-ended and never-ending.

Accordingly, a building exemplifies when it functions like a sample. When it functions within a dense system (like a sample from the sea), then it symbolizes artistically and we speak of a work of architecture. Here one sees again why Goodman's approach is a functional one: depending on the system, a building may or may not be a work of architecture. The range of exemplification in architecture is extremely vast, for potentially all of the possessed properties can be exemplified. There are nevertheless some particularities that allow for a certain grouping according to the features exemplified: form, structure, construction elements, materials, and function. This grouping is neither exhaustive nor exclusive (buildings may simultaneously exemplify other features and symbolize in other ways), but it clarifies how exemplification takes place in architecture. Most importantly, it shows how architecture and architects may contribute to understanding by creating original symbolizations and by rendering salient features that had previously only been possessed. These processes further contribute to worldmaking.

A building can exemplify its form or that of some of its components and any feature related to form: geometrical shapes, planes, lines, horizontality, verticality, undulation, flatness, and so on. Pyramids, pinnacles, obelisks, and roofs exemplify their respective shapes; the Sydney Opera House and the Guggenheim Museum in Bilbao exemplify undulation and curves; the Barcelona Pavilion exemplifies horizontality and the Seagram Building verticality and orthogonal geometry; Palladio's Villa Rotonda exemplifies proportion; some churches exemplify a Latin cross, others a rectangular or a round shape. Zaha Hadid's designs are known for exemplifying their formal traits over any other features and this exploration of form leads buildings to exemplify in unforeseen and unexpected ways.

A building exemplifies its structure when the construction elements that hold up the building are symbolized. This means that structure must be distinguishable from the other non-structural elements of the building, that structure must be a salient feature. This emphasis can be achieved either by making the structure stand out (this is how the Eiffel Tower and Gothic churches exemplify their structures), or by using other construction elements to make the structure salient, as happens in the John Hancock Tower in Chicago. Here the structure is on the skin of the building and clad in a way that prevails over the floors' separations and the disposition of the windows. Specifically, what is seen on the building's façades is not the structure itself, but the cladding that contains the structure, and in this way structure is exemplified.

Goodman's example for exemplification of structure in architecture is Gerrit Rietveld's Schröder House. Basing his view on a passage by William H. Jordy, which states that the linear elements and planes at the house 'make visible the "build" [sic] of the building', Goodman concludes that 'the building is designed to refer effectively to certain characteristics of its structure'(Goodman 1988: 38). The Schröder House, however, exemplifies form rather than structure, because the planes and lines exemplified are not related to the building's structure: these elements do not help in distinguishing bearing walls from partition walls, for instance, but rather make other features salient, such as verticality, hence referring to form.

Both exemplification of form and exemplification of structure seem to imply that form and structure be visible or salient to be exemplified. This, however, cannot be generalized. The structure of a building may be exemplified even though it is not immediately accessible: when entering a Gothic church, for example, one can first overlook its structure and only after careful observation distinguish columns, arches, keystones, and ribs that support the building and then recognize the exemplified structure. The same may happen with form: Borromini's Sant'Ivo alla Sapienza in Rome exemplifies form in a very subtle way, with a complex geometry that underlies the plan and a composition of circles and triangles; only once this is discerned can exemplification of this geometric composition be perceived. Exemplification of form, structure, and any other property does not need to be conspicuous, but can also be subtle and not immediately obvious.

Buildings may exemplify also some of their construction elements, such as walls, doors, windows, roofs, or balconies. Frank Gehry's Stata Center at the Massachusetts Institute of Technology exemplifies some of its windows, as they seem to fall out from their frames. The Centre Georges Pompidou in Paris exemplifies its service elements and renders them salient by placing them outside the building (instead of hiding them in chases or between walls) as well as by colouring the tubes: the air conditioning ducts are blue, the electric conduits yellow, the water pipes green, and the elevator cables red. The Centre Pompidou also exemplifies the staircase, by placing it outside and painting it grey, and the structure, a white steel skeleton from which the floors are suspended. A building can also exemplify some of the elements that were used for its construction, but are no longer parts of the finished building. Such is the case of the marks on the concrete left by the wooden casting elements, necessary to form the wet concrete, that exemplify the wood planks used for construction. Carlo Scarpa's works are a perfect example of this sort of exemplification. Similarly, the casting plug holes, indicating the bolt locations of the form-work, exemplify the casting materials used to mould the concrete, as can be seen in many of Louis Kahn's projects.

Buildings can also exemplify their construction materials (stone, brick, concrete, iron, wood, marble, or glass) and some of the qualities of those materials (a stone's texture, a brick's colour, the concrete's roughness, the iron's weight, the wood's fibrousness, or the glass' transparency). The onyx wall at the Barcelona Pavilion exemplifies the shininess of this kind of quartz, its watermarks, and its smoothness. Peter Zumthor's works are characterized by exemplifying the qualities of wood (colour, texture, fibre marks, warmth). Brutalist architecture is known for exemplifying the un-honed concrete that makes up the building. Some buildings succeed in exemplifying several properties of the same material at once, as happens in the recent addition to Harvard's Science Center by Leers Weinzapfel Associates (Figure 8). The addition's façade is composed of a regular pattern of translucent glass channels and transparent windows. With the different lighting conditions throughout the day (natural daylight and artificial light at night) different qualities of the glass – transparency, translucency, opacity, and reflectivity – are exemplified. These properties are used for further exemplifications: at night, when the artificial lighting inside the building comes through to the exterior, the objects inside create a pattern of shadows which is exemplified. In addition, the glass façade of the Science Center wraps into the interior of the building and there other properties are exemplified: instead of being just a flat surface, now the glass exemplifies its thickness and form.

Figure 8 Science Center at Harvard University. Leers Weinzapfel Associates.

Finally, buildings can exemplify their function. Goodman emphasizes that what is usually considered as 'expression' of function corresponds to 'exemplification' in his terminology, for the function is literally and not metaphorically possessed (Goodman 1988: 41). Recalling previous examples, many buildings that represent a thing also exemplify the function of selling, manufacturing, or containing that thing. Buildings depicting ice creams, hot dogs, burgers, or donuts usually exemplify their function of selling these foods; the picnic-basket building exemplifies the function of manufacturing baskets and a movie theatre with a depicted film reel exemplifies the function of screening movies. In all these cases, exemplification of function occurs through the depiction of something that refers to the building's function. Not all buildings depicting something, however, also exemplify function: the robot building in Bangkok does not exemplify the function of manufacturing robots, nor does the shark building in Silver Spring, Maryland exemplify the function of containing sharks. In these examples, the buildings' functions are not exemplified through what they depict.

Apart from being exemplified through depiction, function can also be exemplified in other ways. A factory exemplifies the function of manufacturing through its industrial chimneys, lifts, big entrances, and huge rooms for holding machinery, so that function is exemplified through some of the building's elements. This, however, cannot be generalized, for buildings may change their function and continue exemplifying their former function, as is the case of factories now functioning as housing or accommodating other activities. Here two options are possible: either the building still exemplifies its former function of manufacturing or the building's function is no longer related to the building's form and, therefore, only form, and not function, is exemplified. Yet in other cases there is no need of any formal feature to exemplify function. Both the Stata Center and the Science Center exemplify the function of being academic buildings, and only the features of the symbol system (such as classifying buildings according to the activity they host) are required to exemplify function. So, form is not a necessary feature to exemplify function; nor is it sufficient: form may be an indicator of a certain function, but this does not mean that the function is exemplified. One can distinguish between an apartment building and a bank because the former has a certain kind of roof, windows, and entrance, and the latter has a big entrance, noble materials, and security elements. These features enable recognition of function but, since exemplification requires both possession and reference, only those buildings that also function as symbols can exemplify function.

The famous modernist motto of 'form follows function' does not necessarily entail a symbolic relationship in Goodman's terms, where it would mean 'form exemplifies function' or 'through form, function is exemplified'. That a building was designed following this principle, or that the architect intended to do so, does not cause form to exemplify function. And even if the forms of a building were following function, independently from what function exactly means, this still does not mean that form symbolizes function.

The famous modernist motto of 'form follows function' does

not necessarily entail a symbolic relationship in Goodman's

terms, where it would mean 'form exemplifies function' or 'through form, function is exemplified'.

Articulation

In most of the cases of exemplification discussed above there seems to be an intermediate element, a feature of the building itself, that enables reference to possessed properties. In the Hancock Tower, exemplification of structure is achieved by putting the structure on the exterior and covering it with a cladding in order to emphasize it. In the Centre Pompidou, the service elements are exemplified by putting them on the façade and painting them in bright colours. In the Harvard Science Center, the features of the glass are exemplified by strategically placing glass panes and channels where the features of the material stand out. These modes of making certain of the building's features stand out are processes of articulation, which can be understood as some sort of joint that structures design elements in a construction (Ching 1995: 52). The purpose of articulation is to bring together the several parts of a building into a whole and, at the same time, make each of these parts stand out; articulation seeks both integration and differentiation. According to this and considering the previous examples, it could seem that articulation is the formal, material, or tectonic condition that buildings must have in order to make exemplification possible. It could seem that a certain kind of articulation of form, structure, construction elements, materials, or function is prior to and necessary for exemplification. Whereas it is true that in these cases a certain degree of articulation enables exemplification, that is, that in these cases articulation functions as an intermediate step between simple possession and reference, articulation is neither a necessary nor a sufficient condition for exemplification. That articulation is a necessary condition for exemplification means that there is no exemplification without articulation; that articulation is a sufficient condition for exemplification means that the presence of articulation guarantees the presence of exemplification. Neither of those is true: Many exemplified features (such as being an academic building or being an original or groundbreaking one) do not require articulation and, on the other hand, the mere presence of articulation does not assure exemplification (the emergency exits of a building are clearly articulated, but not referred to by the building).

Articulation is neither a necessary nor sufficient condition for exemplification, but this does not exclude that articulation plays an important role in the symbolization of a building. In some cases, as with exemplification of structure, it is very difficult to find architectural works that exemplify without articulating. Articulation is a means architects have to emphasize some of the building's features and in that way suggest possible features that could be exemplified; it is a way architects have to prompt symbolization and to bring about interpretations. In addition, articulation is an element to be taken into account when interpreting and evaluating works of architecture: two buildings may exemplify the same features and one may be more successful that the other in exemplifying them because of their articulations.

Articulation is a means architects have to emphasize some of the building's features and in that way suggest possible features that could be exemplified; it is a way architects have to prompt symbolization and to bring about interpretations.

Expression

Like denotation, exemplification can be literal or metaphorical. All the cases discussed above were cases of literal exemplification. An environmentally friendly building that exemplifies being a green building is a case of metaphorical exemplification. If in addition it were painted green, it would also literally exemplify being a green building. When metaphorical exemplification occurs within an artistic symbol system, Goodman terms it expression (Goodman 1968: 85). Expression is thus a mode of reference that should not be mistaken with the manifestation of an artist's feelings or the emotions awoken in the viewer. A work of art or architecture can certainly express feelings and emotions, but also any other metaphorical property. To understand how expression works in architecture, it is first necessary to briefly discuss metaphors and metaphorical exemplification. Note that Goodman's account of metaphor (Goodman 1968: 68–95; Goodman 1976: 102–7; Goodman 1979; Goodman 1984: 71–7; Elgin 1983: 59–70; Elgin 1996: 53–72; Elgin 1997b: 197–204) is not the only philosophical explanation of metaphors and that his discussion of metaphors is opposed to other accounts (Davidson 1978; Fogelin 1988).

In a metaphorical manner, Goodman describes metaphor as a 'matter of teaching an old word new tricks – of applying an old label in a new way', as 'an affair between a predicate with a past and an object that yields while protesting', and as 'a calculated category mistake – or rather as a happy and revitalizing, even if bigamous, second marriage' (Goodman 1968: 69, 73). In a metaphorical transfer the label carries out a new function, so that metaphors are understood as moonlighting (Goodman 1978: 104; Goodman 1984: 71). A metaphor is thus the application of a literal label with an established use to an object that does not belong to this literal application. This new use is guided by the prior literal one and, at the same time, creates a certain tension and conflict. By interpreting the elements of the symbol system, one determines which metaphorical use of a certain term is at play in each context. The label 'green', for instance, literally sorts out things that are of green colour, and metaphorically it may differentiate buildings that are environmentally friendly from more contaminating ones, envious from non-envious people, or immature projects from ready ones. The application of 'green' to environmentally friendly buildings is established through referential chains and is based on the prior literal application of 'green' to nature and the natural environment, and the application of 'green' to immature projects is based on the literal application of 'green' to unripe fruits. Through interpretation we know that 'green' refers to environmentally friendly in a context and to immature in another. And even though we may not know the origin of the relation between green and envy, this does not hinder metaphorical usage. The metaphorical use of labels depends on the literal one, but the demarcation line between them changes. When the novelty and vivacity of a metaphor vanishes and its application becomes customary, then the metaphor becomes familiar and freezes. The initial tension that occurs when applying a literal term to a new object disappears: colours are metaphorically warm or cold, notes are metaphorically high or low, but the metaphor is no longer vivid (Goodman 1968: 68).

Metaphors have their own truth value, which is determined by the symbol system to which the metaphor belongs: 'The White House is a green building' is literally and metaphorically false, because it is neither painted green nor it is environmentally friendly; 'My cousin's farm is a green building' is literally false and metaphorically true, because it is ochre and environmentally friendly. So, one can determine the truth value of a metaphor in the same way that one can determine whether the use of a literal label is true or false: by interpreting the label and its application within a symbol system. In addition to their own truth value, metaphors have cognitive value and an explanatory power that literal expressions lack. Metaphors contribute to the economy of language insofar as they allow the use of the same terms in different contexts. This, however, does not entail a limitation in our ways of expressing things, but rather a creative process that establishes new associations and points out aspects that maybe otherwise would not take place. The metaphor 'green building' sorts out environmentally friendly buildings and the expression 'this building is greener than that one' provides a novel organization within environmentally friendly buildings. Metaphors are not susceptible to being completely translated into literal paraphrases, so that new metaphorical classifications may offer a genuine contribution to understanding. As with literal symbols, some metaphors are more successful than others in providing new insights and novel organizations, but this does not mean that unsuccessful metaphors lack cognitive value: they may be banal, commonplace, or point to certain features that are plainly false. Like all other symbols, metaphors can be evaluated; they can be assessed, are open to interpretation, and subject to consensus.

Metaphors are not susceptible to being completely translated into literal paraphrases, so that new metaphorical

classifications may offer a genuine contribution to understanding.

Whereas metaphorical denotation consists of applying a metaphorical label to something, metaphorical exemplification requires the reference to a metaphorically possessed property. A building metaphorically exemplifies being a green building when it possesses the property of being green in the sense of environmentally friendly and further reference is established. As with literal exemplification, just being a green building is not enough to symbolize, reference within a symbol system is required. Note also that to possess a metaphorical property does not mean that it is not a true possession:

> **Metaphorical possession is indeed not *literal* possession; but possession is actual whether metaphorical or literal.**
>
> (Goodman 1968: 68)

No matter how difficult or easy it may be to detect metaphorical properties, this does not mean that they are not actual properties. As with metaphorical denotation, a symbol metaphorically exemplifies depending on prior literal usage and, as with literal properties, metaphorical properties are not arbitrary, but are subject to verification. A house can only exemplify being metaphorically green if it actually is environmentally friendly, low-energy consuming, or non-polluting, among others. If it is a building that does not fulfil any of the requirements to be environmentally friendly, then it does not possess the metaphorical property of being green and thus does not exemplify such property. Affirming that a building is metaphorically green does not make a building become green. Only stipulation is not enough; possession and further reference are necessary for exemplification, both literal and metaphorical.

The difference between metaphorical exemplification and expression is that the latter occurs within artistic symbol systems and the former does not. This does not exclude that one and the same symbol can both metaphorically exemplify and express some of its properties. Symbols can be multi-referential and symbolize the same or different properties in many ways at the same time. After undergoing a renovation to reduce its energy consumption, the Empire State Building was lit up in green: the skyscraper literally exemplified being green, it metaphorically exemplified being green, and expressed being a green building. This very same green light, however, does not only symbolize these: the Empire State Building has been lit green to celebrate the end of Ramadan, to honour the Robin Hood Foundation, and in honour of Earth Day. Interpretation is necessary to determine what is symbolized and what symbolization processes take place.

Expression as a way of referring is explained resorting to metaphor and exemplification, but it is not simply the conjunction of metaphor and exemplification that occurs in an artistic symbol system. A building can function as a metaphor and exemplify without expressing: the Taj Mahal is a metaphor for profound love and exemplifies the marble it is made of, but it does not express either of them. Defining expression as reference to actually possessed metaphorical properties entails that any feelings, emotions, or any other metaphorical property are found in the symbol itself, not in the artist or the viewer. It also entails that there is not a causal relation between that emotion and the artist, the audience or the work's content: an artist does not have to feel sadness to express it, an actor does not have to be sad to express sadness, and a work does not need to represent or describe a sad scene to express such a feeling. So,

> [a] building may express feelings it does not feel, ideas it cannot think or state, activities it cannot perform.
>
> (Goodman 1988: 40)

And it can do so independently from the feelings of creator and audience, ideas, and activities, because it actually possesses those metaphorical properties. As with exemplification, the architect can employ certain mechanisms, such as articulation, that can make a building suitable to express certain properties, although this does not imply a causal relation between mechanism and expressed property, nor that this architectural way will succeed in expressing a certain property. Furthermore, a building can express without having been designed to do so. As with exemplification, articulation is neither necessary nor sufficient to achieve expression but it is nevertheless an architectural means to prompt expression. There are innumerable metaphorical properties that can be expressed and sometimes expression is achieved through other modes of symbolization. Without aiming to be exhaustive, the following examples show different ways in which buildings may express.

the architect can employ certain mechanisms, such as articulation, that can make a building suitable to express certain properties

Goodman's example of an expressing building is the Vierzehnheiligen Basilica in Bavaria, which expresses syncopation and dynamism. The church spaces are not literally playing music or moving, but rather its organization is metaphorically syncopated and dynamic. In this case, the metaphorical transfer of these two labels is suggested by certain exemplified properties of the building that Goodman identifies in the basilica's vault, which is not a 'single undulating shell but … a smooth shape interrupted by others' (Goodman 1988: 40). Like a musical syncopation, which is a displacement of an accent from a strong beat to a weak one that produces an effect of shifting back or anticipating the accent, the vault is interrupted by other vaults that accentuate certain parts of the vault that otherwise would remain in the background, and in that way an unexpected rhythm is created. Similarly, the dynamism is achieved by the combination of undulating forms, sinuous shapes, and by opening up spaces of different sizes to each other. In the Vierzehnheiligen Basilica expression is achieved through exemplification. This, however, cannot be generalized, because otherwise only buildings that exemplify could express. Or even more, the buildings exemplifying the same properties as the Basilica of Vierzehnheiligen should also express syncopation and dynamism. There is no causal relation between certain literal properties that are exemplified and certain metaphorical properties that are expressed. As is shown below, there are plentiful cases where expression is involved with other kinds of symbolization, others where expression occurs independently of other modes of reference, and others in which expression is possible precisely because certain properties are merely possessed and not exemplified.

There is no causal relation between certain literal properties that are exemplified and certain metaphorical properties that are expressed.

The Dunmore Pavilion is an example of expression by means of representation (Figure 9). The dome in the centre of this folly is shaped as a pineapple, hence representing this tropical fruit. But it also expresses power and wealth, for it metaphorically possesses these properties. The metaphorical transfer can be explained as follows: pineapples were considered a rare delicacy when they first arrived to Europe and only the wealthy could afford them. Pineapples thus symbolize being exotic, expensive, and exclusive. By representing a pineapple,

Figure 9 Dunmore Pavilion, The Pineapple, Scotland.

the wealth and power of those who had access to pineapples is expressed. An actual pineapple does not symbolize power and wealth; it is just a pineapple. It is rather the representation of the pineapple that enables the expression of power and wealth. Other features of the building also express these properties. The pineapple is a modification of the classical dome with a cupola: the upper leaves of the pineapple are represented in a way that their shape forms that of a cupola. According to the symbol system of architectural typologies, a dome is a symbol of power and wealth. Hence, the dome and the cupola, regardless of the fact that they are shaped as a pineapple, also express power and wealth. It is arguable whether power and wealth are expressed by means of the exemplification of form, or whether the simple presence of dome and cupola, i.e., that the building merely possesses them, suffices for expression. One possible interpretation is that since dome and cupola represent a pineapple, expression of power and wealth is reinforced by the fact that the pineapple is also a dome and not because cupola and dome are exemplified. Another element that expresses power and wealth is the main entrance to the pavilion, just under the dome, which represents a classic Palladian entrance. As with the dome, the entrance functions as a symbol within a system of architectural typologies that establishes that this classical element in this case symbolizes power and wealth. Finally, power is also expressed by means of exemplification of a phallic form. The entrance together with the dome and the drum clearly stand out from the rest of the building: whereas the pavilion is made of brown brick, the entrance and the dome are made of white stone; and the horizontality of the one-story pavilion helps in emphasizing the verticality of its central elements. The Dunmore Pavilion thus expresses the same features through at least three different ways: by the representation of a pineapple, by the presence of a classical dome and entrance, and by the exemplification of a phallic form.

In other cases, expression occurs in a variety of ways. Daniel Libeskind's extension of the Jewish Museum in Berlin expresses a whole range of metaphorical properties through a series of architectural devices that are sometimes combined also with other modes of symbolization (Figure 10). According to Libeskind, the building has the shape of an irregular zigzag that

Figure 10 Jewish Museum, Berlin. Daniel Libeskind.

symbolizes a deconstructed and distorted Star of David: through exemplification of a star that has been taken apart, the broken history of the Jewish people is expressed. This zigzag is crossed by a void space that slices linearly through the entire building. This intertwinement results in five empty spaces or voids that rise vertically from the ground floor of the building up to the roof and that interrupt the continuity of the building's zigzag. Or, the other way around, the void space is continuously interrupted by the building. The voids do not feature exhibitions, their walls are made of bare concrete, lack climatization, and are largely without artificial light; all of these separate the voids from the rest of the building. This creates a spatial gap that exemplifies emptiness and expresses other properties. Primarily, the void, as an absence that is continuously present throughout the museum, expresses the absence of Berlin's Jews in a particular period of the history of the city.

A visit to the museum begins in an underground entrance accessible from an already existing Baroque building. By connecting both buildings, the belonging of Jewish history to the overall history of the city is expressed.

From the entrance a corridor begins: it is the Axis of Continuity, which is cut through by the Axis of Emigration and the Axis of the Holocaust, expressing two events that interrupted the path of the Jewish people and also symbolizing the connection between the three realities of Jewish life in Germany. The Axis of the Holocaust is a corridor that becomes ever narrower and darker and comes to a dead end – the Holocaust Tower, or the so-called 'voided void'. The tower is a windowless space with no entrance except from the underground level. As the other void spaces, it is neither heated nor cooled, and its only light comes from a small slit in its roof. The visitor accesses the tower through a heavy metal door and, once inside, the echoing of one's own steps and, farther away, exterior sounds and light can be perceived. The Holocaust Tower expresses various properties. Libeskind says that it stands for (and in Goodman's terms, expresses) 'humanity reduced to ashes' (Libeskind and Binet 1999: 30). It also expresses fear, desolation, loss, panic, separation of the outside world, or the impossibility of escape. It may express many other metaphorically possessed features; visitors experiencing and interpreting the building may discover properties that had not been realized before. The Axis of Emigration is an ascending corridor with an uneven floor and slightly slanted walls that leads outside to daylight, to the Garden of Exile, only accessible after crossing a heavy door. This axis expresses the arduous way towards exile, symbolized by the garden, which is a perfect square with square columns that create a geometrical grid. The ground, however, is slanted so that, without visually perceiving it, it directly affects one's sense of balance. Thus the garden expresses safety but at the same time disorientation and instability, features common to the situation of all the Jews who either emigrated or fled into exile. The combination of straight walls, the labyrinth-like structure, and the uneven ground suggests the expression of these conflicting features. The garden can also express hope, tranquillity, or relief. Others maintain that the whole museum, and particularly the garden, expresses the uncanny, especially in the German literal sense of the term: the 'Unheimlichkeit', the impossibility of finding a home or 'Heim', the impossibility of settling down (Young 2000: 154). Finally, the Axis of Continuity is the longest corridor of the three. It is a tilted walkway that leads up to the exhibition levels and the void, expressing the continuation of Berlin's history. The Axis is transformed to stairs that do not end at the exhibition level, but continue up until they reach a wall, and thus the fact that history does not finish is symbolized. The staircase is traversed by a series of slanted trusses and also by beams of light that enter through the irregular apertures in the wall that are more slits than windows, expressing difficulties and obstacles in the history of the Jewish people.

The general structure of the museum is not perceptible: the exhibition halls are irregular in shape; the reflective zinc-clad façade barely enables one to discern the structure of the building's interior, for the divisions of neither levels nor rooms are distinguishable from the outside; and the zigzag cut through the void is only visible from a bird's-eye view, or through the building's plan. Overall, then, the museum expresses disorientation and disruption and, precisely because of the successful expression of these properties, the building can be said to poorly fulfil its practical function as a museum. The strictly linear curatorial path through the exhibition is at odds with the museum's fragmented composition; the museum does not exemplify its organization at all and this lack of clarity must be mitigated by indicating the visitor's way with a series of stickers with arrows on the floor. The Jewish Museum may express many other properties and, evidently, it symbolizes many other features in other ways. In some cases, features are being exemplified or represented to further be expressed (as with the fragmented Star of David), and in others expression is possible precisely because a certain feature is not exemplified: the tilted ground that provokes the visitor's unbalance at the Garden of Exile is not exemplified; if it were, disorientation, instability, and the uncanny would not be expressed. What a building expresses needs to be interpreted. The presence of certain features is not enough to make the building function as a symbol, nor are specific features necessarily correlated to certain expressed properties. Darkness and narrowness do not directly imply expression of desolation and fear, as they do in the museum; bedrooms may be dark and narrow and, if they symbolize at all, they most probably do not refer to desolation and fear, but rather cosiness and safety.

What a building expresses needs to be interpreted. The

presence of certain features is not enough to make the

building function as a symbol, nor are specific features

necessarily correlated to certain expressed properties.

Other modes of reference

Apart from denotation, exemplification, and expression, there are multiple and indirect ways of symbolizing, the main ones being allusion, variation, and style. Whereas the first three are direct modes of reference, i.e., they entail one-step referential relations, multiple and indirect ways of reference are constituted by a combination of the simple modes of reference through more or less complex chains of reference. Allusion, variation, and style show particularities that allow for distinction among each other.

Allusion

Allusion is a 'form of referential action at a distance. One thing alludes to another by referring to it indirectly' (Elgin 1983: 142; see also Goodman 1984: 65–6; Goodman 1988: 42–3, 70; Elgin 1983: 142–6; Ross 1981). Allusion must not be mistaken with evocation. Whereas allusion is a mode of reference, evocation consists of the production of a feeling, emotion, or idea that does not necessarily entail a referential relation. A certain building in my hometown can evoke nostalgia in me, but it does not need to allude to nostalgia; another building can allude to nostalgia without evoking, and yet another one can both evoke and allude to nostalgia (Goodman 1984: 65). The indirect relation in allusion is established via chains of reference that involve denotation and exemplification, both literal and metaphorical. These chains vary in complexity, but generally begin with one of two basic ones, which Elgin describes as follows: "*a* alludes *b* by denoting something *c* that exemplifies *b*" and "*a* alludes *b* by exemplifying something *c* that denotes *b*" (Elgin 1983: 142).

Allusion must not be mistaken with evocation.

Taking Goodman's examples, the first chain of allusion occurs when Robert Venturi talks about 'contradiction' in architecture (Goodman 1988: 42, Venturi 1966). 'Contradiction' (*a*) alludes to the inconsistency and incongruity of a particular architectural design (*b*) by denoting those sentences (*c*) that exemplify being inconsistent and incongruent and these properties are also exemplified by a building (*b*). The second sort of chain takes place when a building such as the Vanna Venturi House (*a*) alludes to contradiction (*b*) by exemplifying certain forms (*c*) that are denoted by the label 'contradiction' (*b*). The Vanna Venturi House exemplifies an array of opposed features: the house is 'both complex and simple, open and closed, big and little' and there is also a lack of correspondence between inside and outside (Venturi 1966: 118). This mode of symbolization is not direct, for the Vanna Venturi House does not literally or metaphorically possess the property of being contradictory, but rather alludes to contradiction, thus symbolizing indirectly.

The chains of reference that explain allusion are similar to the ones that explain metaphorical transfers. In some cases allusion even intervenes in one step of the metaphorical referential chain. The difference lies in that a metaphorical term recalls the literal application of this term, whereas allusion does not. Allusion only requires joint exemplification and denotation of certain properties without differentiating between literal and metaphorical properties. So, while a metaphorical chain links the literal to the metaphorical application of a term, a chain of reference in allusion links any kind of property. These chains are generally much longer than the ones discussed above and their intermediate steps do not need to be obvious; since there may be multiple chains that explain the same allusion, the discussed chains should be considered schematic bridges rather than the only way to establish a relation of allusion. There is no pre-established limit on the length of the referential chain of allusion. There are no logically prior limits to what a symbol can allude to, but there may be some pragmatic limits: if a certain referential chain is so long, complicated, and abstruse that the relation from symbol to the alluded thing cannot be discerned, then allusion does not occur. An overview of the chain is necessary to establish the connection between the symbol that alludes and what is alluded to. Sometimes the overview may depend on one's knowledge: only those who know about the Sydney Opera House and the manga cartoon Dragon Ball can establish a connection between the two and interpret the Sydney Opera House as alluding to Son Goku's hair. The limits of allusion are thus pragmatic, not theoretical.

Not all chains of reference constitute allusion:

> **Gaudí's famous church in Barcelona refers to a certain building, not to the mountains that that building refers to.**
>
> (Goodman 1988: 42–3)

These chains are not reversible and, like representation, allusion is not symmetrical: that a certain building alludes to Greek temples does not imply that Greek temples allude to that building. Similarly to copies or reproductions, when a building alludes to certain features of other buildings, this does not necessarily entail that all the features that those other buildings symbolize are also symbolized by the alluding building. And, in case they are symbolized, they do not need to be symbolized in the same way. The several copies of the Eiffel Tower represent the Eiffel Tower and they may allude to France. But whereas the Eiffel Tower in Paris exemplifies the centennial of the French Revolution, the Eiffel Tower in Las Vegas alludes to it. So, apart from representing an original, copies refer to some features the original symbolizes via allusion.

In addition to alluding to certain labels or properties (such as contradiction in the case of the Vanna Venturi House and to France in the case of the copies of the Eiffel Tower), works of architecture can allude to purportedly possessed properties, to other works of art and architecture, and also to certain styles, artists, or genres. The several instances of trompe-l'oeil found in buildings allude to certain properties that the building purports to possess. The painted dome at the Baroque church of Sant'Ignazio di Loyola in Rome alludes to this architectural structure and shape via a chain of reference that involves exemplification of certain features through the representation of a dome. Some have proposed another mode of reference, termed 'suggestion', for the cases

67 BUILDINGS AS SYMBOLS

of symbolization of purportedly possessed properties, such as the trompe-l'oeil and the false perspective of Greek temples (Lagueux 1998). However, these cases can already be accounted for through the mode of allusion, hence the introduction of suggestion as a new mode of reference is an unnecessary complication to Goodman's system.

> Moreover, allusion has nothing to do with temporality, for it does not only take place between contemporary works or between present works alluding to the past. Allusion to the future is also possible: futurist architecture alludes to the future, even though this future is unknown.

Allusion to other works of art and architecture as well as to certain periods or styles is a constant symbolization resource in both architecture and art. It is said that the front façade of the Vanna Venturi House alludes to Michelangelo's Porta Pia in Rome (Moos 1987: 244). Similarly, the Pantheon in Rome is alluded to by Palladio's Villa Rotonda, Soufflot's Pantheon in Paris, Thomas Jefferson's Rotunda at the University of Virginia, or McKim, Mead, and White's Low Memorial Library at Columbia University. As with any other mode of symbolization, what a building alludes to is determined through interpretation. The more one knows about architecture, the more allusions one is able to detect. Allusion is not related to the architect's intentions: even though Palladio, Soufflot, and Jefferson were inspired by the Pantheon in Rome when designing their works, this is neither a necessary nor a sufficient condition for allusion. At most, knowing these facts may serve as a clue to determine whether these buildings actually allude to the Pantheon in Rome. Moreover, allusion has nothing to do with temporality, for it does not only take place between contemporary works or between present works alluding to the past. Allusion to the future is also possible: futurist architecture alludes to the future, even though this future is unknown.

Allusion can be ironic. The Vanna Venturi House can be interpreted as ironically alluding to the strict and traditional separation of architectural styles by combining elements of several styles in the same building. In that way, Venturi is mocking the architectural canon. When symbolization is ironic, the referential chain is much more complex and it may include other allusions and figurative denotation and exemplification. Specifically, what is figuratively possessed may be the opposite, an exaggeration or an understatement of the literal feature, which is what happens when a skyscraper is called 'tiny' (Goodman 1988: 71). This process also takes place when the Vanna Venturi House refers to several architectural styles by exaggerating their paradigmatic forms: the façade is dominated by an oversized pediment recalling those of Greek temples, the strip-windows on the right recall the type of windows commonly employed by Modernist architects, and these windows contrast with another oversized divided light window on the façade, which recalls the traditional New England windows. Understatement of a literal feature also occurs in the Vanna Venturi House: above an outsized square door with an enlarged lintel there is a relief of an arch (not a real arch). The combination of a huge square and lintel with a barely traced arch enables the ironic allusion. Irony is thus a special case of allusion; it is a complex form of indirect reference with the particularity that that which the symbol alludes to is the opposite, an exaggeration, an understatement, or in general a contrast of a certain literal feature of the alluded thing.

Variation

The paradigmatic case of variation in the arts is found in music, where a variation upon a theme is a creative modification of a given melody that presents the theme in a new but still recognizable way. Goodman examines this complex referential relation in music to then extrapolate it to other arts in 'Variations on Variation – or Picasso back to Bach' (Goodman 1988: 66–81; see also D'Orey 1999: 515–29). A variation is related to a theme in that it exemplifies some of the musical features of that theme and precisely these exemplified features are what relate variation and theme. Simply exemplifying is not enough, for a piece may exemplify the same rhythm as another piece and not be its variation. The exemplified rhythm has to be also the feature that relates both theme and variation. This relation can either be direct or indirect, i.e., via exemplification or via allusion of common or contrasted features. A variation, for instance, can contrastively exemplify a theme by exemplifying being in a minor key, whereas the theme exemplifies being in a major key. Goodman establishes two conditions for variation: a 'formal' and a 'functional' one:

> First, to be *eligible* as a variation, a passage must be like the theme in certain respects and contrast with it in certain others. Second, to *function* as a variation, an eligible passage must literally exemplify the requisite shared, and metaphorically exemplify the requisite contrasting, features of the theme, and refer to it via these features.
>
> (Goodman 1988: 71–2, his emphasis)

It is thus the symbolic functioning that makes a piece be a variation upon a theme. And, as with aesthetic symbolic functioning, this does not need to be permanent: certain works that usually do not function as a variation may function as such under certain circumstances, as happens when copies function as variations of an original work or when a series of initially unrelated paintings function as variations upon a common theme when being part of the same exhibition (Goodman 1988: 75–6). In this last case, the referential relation may include other modes of symbolization, such as denotation and representation, but the requirements for being a variation remain the same.

The cases of variation in architecture can be classified depending on whether they are variations upon an architectural theme or work, variations upon a form, and variations upon a style or an unspecified theme. The first case occurs when the basis for the variation is a particular building or structural element. The several buildings that allude to the Pantheon in Rome can also be considered as variations upon it. So the Low Memorial Library exemplifies the Pantheon's dome and the portico with columns, but it does not possess nor exemplify all of the Pantheon's features: whereas the pediment at the Pantheon is triangular, the library's one is rectangular; whereas the Pantheon has Corinthian columns, the library has Ionic columns; size and materials are also different. These contrasting properties that the library possesses and the Pantheon lacks are exemplified and contrastively referred to by the library, which allows considering the library as a variation upon the Pantheon in Rome. Another example of the first kind is that of the several variations upon Solomonic columns, the helical columns characterized by a spiralling twisting shaft like a corkscrew. These variations are particularly interesting because their original theme is no longer extant, so that the architectural variations were initially based upon the biblical descriptions of the two columns that flanked the entrance to the Temple of Solomon in Jerusalem and further upon the several built variations of such columns, as Trajan's Column, the Columns of Constantine, or the columns at Bernini's baldachin in Saint Peter's Basilica in Rome, and also upon the various Solomonic columns depicted in paintings. Since the variation crosses through different artistic disciplines and media, variations upon Solomonic columns are a kind of cross-modal variation. Finally, copies may function as variations inasmuch as they symbolize some features and contrastively symbolize some others: the Eiffel Tower in Las Vegas exemplifies the same form as the one in Paris while contrastively exemplifying its size.

The cases of variation in architecture can be classified depending on whether they are variations upon an architectural theme or work, variations upon a form, and variations upon a style or an unspecified theme.

The second kind of variation in architecture, variation upon a form, occurs when the basis of the variation is not a particular building but one of its formal features. The variations upon the traditional Latin cross plan of churches are a clear example. The basic form, or theme, consists of a Latin cross plan where one arm of the cross forms the church's nave and the chancel, and the other arm perpendicular to it forms the transept. This form may undergo a series of modifications and, if both common and contrastive features are symbolized, then these modifications can be understood as variations. The initial Latin cross plan can be redesigned by adding lateral naves adjacent to the central one, by adding an ambulatory and lateral chapels to the chancel with a simple apse, or by modifying the transepts and the naves with lateral chapels and apses. Variation occurs when there is a referential relation that links the Latin cross form to these other forms via reference of possessed and contrastively possessed features. The referential relation between theme and variation is not necessarily related to the historical evolution of this form. Although the transformation of the Latin cross plan is actually a historical one, this does not imply that all variations upon a form are like that or that the evolution of forms always goes from simple to sophisticated.

Finally, there can be variations upon a style or an unspecified theme. As there are variations upon Solomonic columns even though it is unknown how they exactly looked, there can be variations upon certain features that characterize a certain style without a given original theme, so that the variations refer to each other with reference to common shared and contrastively shared features. This is what happens at Columbia University's Morningside campus, where its main buildings can be interpreted as variations of each other. These buildings are all the same size, are made out of brick, have a green copper roof, the same number of windows and doors framed with white stone, but they also differ from each other in a subtle way. The corners of the buildings have different patterns: some of the stones are all the same size, others combine stones of two sizes creating a zipper, others have stones with slightly rounded corners, and others yet have sculpted stones with different motifs. A similar thing occurs with the window and door frames, which are either single or double, with a decorated lintel or with columns of different orders. All these differences can be interpreted as variations insofar as all the buildings exemplify certain common features and at the same time refer to contrastive features. Since there is no particular building that serves as a theme for the other buildings and there is no way to specify how a building functioning as a theme would be, each building should be understood as a variation upon another variation or as a variation upon or within a certain style (here the Beaux-Arts style), which is what all the variations have in common.

Style

Style as a mode of complex reference has to be understood not as a definition of what constitutes an artistic style (Lang 1987), but rather as a mode of symbolization that accounts for the features that are relevant when establishing what constitutes a style, such as constancy, stability, regularity, repetition, but also change, modification, and relativity. Goodman discusses all this in his essay 'The Status of Style' (Goodman 1978: 23–41; see also D'Orey 1999: 538–58). Style implies in the first place the symbolization of certain properties which are 'characteristic of author, period, place, or school' (Goodman 1978: 35). Style should not be mistaken with signature. Whereas style can count as one of the signature features, one that helps in attributing a work to a certain author, school, or period, not all signature features are stylistic: archival information, excavation reports, and chemical analysis of pigments may help in identifying a work, but they are not a matter of style. For signature features to count as stylistic they need to be symbolized by the work. Stylistic properties are the ones that help us to place the work in a broader artistic context and to associate works among each other; they 'help us answer the questions: who? when? where?' (Goodman 1978: 34). The response is not unique, but admits degrees of generalization. So, Frank Gehry's Stata Center is in Gehry's style, in Gehry's late 1990s and 2000s style, in turn of the millennium style, in the deconstructivist style, in computer-based design style, in Western style, and so on. Style is thus a particular form of classifying works of art and architecture and at the same time a work can be classified under various styles.

Style implies in the first place the symbolization of certain properties which are 'characteristic of author, period, place, or school' (Goodman 1978: 35). Style should not be mistaken with signature.

Perception of style differs from featuring style.

Stylistic features are not limited to formal features, which are generally exemplified, but may also include other kinds of features symbolized in other ways. It is the symbolization of all these features that constitutes style. Both Gothic and neo-Gothic buildings exemplify certain formal features that are constitutive of these styles, such as pointed arches, visible structure and materials, or stained glass windows, but they are not in the same style because they diverge in other symbolized features. Whereas buildings in Gothic style express majesty, the glory of God, and the power of the Church, neo-Gothic buildings may express nostalgia for the past, an upsurge of Christian belief, and also state institutions; and whereas Gothic buildings do not allude to neo-Gothic buildings, the inverse does happen indeed. That style is an identificatory element is not related to the factual process of identifying a certain style. The first refers to the fact that a certain work symbolizes certain stylistic features; the second is related to one's capacity and knowledge to determine a particular style. That one is unable to distinguish between Gothic and neo-Gothic does not mean that there is no such difference. The more one knows, the more subtleties one is able to distinguish and the more precise the classification of style. On the other hand, sometimes one single feature suffices to differentiate between styles or to determine that one building is not of a certain style: churches with pointed arches are not Romanesque and churches with round arches are not Gothic. Perception of style differs from featuring style.

Goodman's account of style as a series of symbolized stylistic features can also be understood in terms of symbol systems, so that stylistic categories belong to a stylistic framework with semantic and syntactic characteristics (Hellmann 1977). As with any other symbol, one work can belong to more than one system and thus be classified under different styles. In this way, changes in a work's style are explained either by changes in the symbol system it is part of or by the insertion of the work to a new symbol system. The Gehry style, for example, will probably be altered with new buildings by the architect. That stylistic systems are open to modification also explains how misattributions of style and further corrections occur. When several paintings by Van Meegeren were mistakenly considered as Vermeer's, the Vermeer style symbol system was altered and new features were considered as part of Vermeer's style. When it was discovered that the paintings by Van Meegeren were fakes, the stylistic features symbolized by them ceased being part of the Vermeer style.

Hence, style as a multiple and complex mode of symbolization or as a special kind of symbol system accounts for both constancy and change of styles. Stylistic features are constant because they are continuously referred to within a symbol system, and they change whenever there is a shift in the features that are symbolized. Constancy and change in symbolization depend on the context, be it social or cultural, and may evolve historically. Style is also an element to consider when interpreting and evaluating a work, even though it does not suffice to understand the whole work, nor it is a guarantee for good quality.

Evaluation and criteria of rightness

In both this and the previous chapter, it has been stressed that symbols are open to many equally right interpretations and that the way to determine whether an interpretation is correct is to contrast it with the symbol's features, the symbol system, and also by taking into account what else is symbolized. Interpretation is thus a matter of fit, 'of some sort of good fit – fit of the parts together and of the whole to context and background' (Goodman 1988: 46). The rightness of an interpretation has thus to do with its adequacy or fitness rather than with truth or falsity. In this sense, works of architecture are not true or false, as may be a declarative proposition or sentence, but rather their symbolization is right or wrong, fair or unfair, in relation to a symbol system and within a given context. Rightness is a relative notion that includes 'standards of acceptability that sometimes supplement or even compete with truth where it applies, or replace truth for nondeclarative renderings' (Goodman 1978: 110). To assess the rightness of architecture's symbolization there is not a detailed list of features, but rather an open-ended series of indications that may help in the evaluation and, plainly speaking, determine whether an architectural work is good or bad.

First of all, buildings rightly symbolize when they enable projectibility and extrapolation, as happens with a model house that perfectly refers to the features that are to be found in the houses built after it. Secondly, buildings rightly symbolize when they are representative, when they symbolize features that make them good exemplars of a certain style or conception. Le Corbusier's Villa Savoye is a right symbol in this sense, because it clearly shows his five points of architecture – the basis of his formulation of modernism and found in many of his other works. On the other hand, his Villa Citrohan certainly contains and is built following these five points, but it does not refer to them in such a proper way and thus it is not as good as the Villa Savoye in being an exemplar of Le Corbusier's principles. And yet the Villa Stein-de-Monzie perfectly exemplifies some points, the stripped windows for instance, but not others, showing that there are degrees of rightness. Third, buildings may rightly symbolize when referring to features that had previously only been possessed, as happens in the Centre Pompidou in its symbolizing of the building's service elements. Fourth, buildings rightly symbolize when they refer to features in a new way or through innovative articulations. Such is the case of the addition of Harvard's Science Center, where the original play with glass allows for the symbolization of the material's different qualities throughout the day. Finally, buildings rightly symbolize when the features to which they refer contribute to the advancement of understanding. This is the case of Le Corbusier's Carpenter Center at Harvard University or the Maison du Brésil in the Cité Université in Paris, whose windows symbolize musical rhythm through a visible and not audible structure: the spatial symbolization of rhythm provides a novel understanding of this musical notion. Novelty, originality, and innovation are also relevant criteria in some cases. The Centre Pompidou was one of the first buildings to symbolize the utility elements by making the building inside out. If today a building would articulate these elements in such a way, it would symbolize them, but this symbolization would not be as successful, for it would not refer to these features for the first time or in a new way, nor it would contribute to the reconfiguration or the advancement of understanding.

To assess the rightness of architecture's symbolization there is

not a detailed list of features, but rather an open-ended series of indications that may help in the evaluation and, plainly speaking, determine whether an architectural work is good or bad.

Similar criteria apply for articulation. First, articulation is right when it contributes to the correct symbolization of a certain property. In the Hancock Tower, structure is rightly articulated by making it clearly distinguishable from the rest of the building. On the other hand, curvature and smoothness at the Guggenheim Museum in Bilbao are rightly symbolized precisely because the articulation is proper. The rightness of articulation varies depending on the property and on the building. Second, novelty and originality of articulation, as happens at Harvard's Science Center, is another factor to consider. Lastly, the success of an articulation may lie in the detail and accuracy of the construction, which is what may make one building's symbolization more adequate than another's.

Again: When is architecture? The symptoms of the aesthetic

Once symbols, symbol systems, and the several modes of reference have been discussed, the question of 'When is architecture?' can be addressed anew. Whereas the initial answer was that something is architecture when it functions as an aesthetic symbol, now a more precise response, even though not definitive, is at hand. To identify when a building functions as a work of art or architecture Goodman resorts to the so-called symptoms of the aesthetic. He first proposed four symptoms of the aesthetic (Goodman 1968: 252–5) and later added one more (Goodman 1978: 67–70; see also Goodman 1984: 135–48 and Elgin 1983: 83–4):

(1) syntactic density, where the finest differences in certain respects constitute a difference between symbols ...; (2) semantic density, where

> symbols are provided for things distinguished by the finest differences
> in certain respects ...; (3) relative repleteness, where comparatively many
> aspects of a symbol are significant ...; (4) exemplification, where a symbol,
> whether or not it denotes, symbolizes by serving as a sample of properties
> it literally or metaphorically possesses; and finally (5) multiple and complex
> reference, where a symbol performs several integrated and interacting
> referential functions, some direct and some mediated through other
> symbols.
>
> (Goodman 1978: 67–8)

A painting is syntactically dense whereas an architectural plan is syntactically disjoint, for a minimal difference may alter the symbolization of a painting but not that of a plan. The English language is semantically dense as opposed to a notation, which is semantically disjoint: whereas linguistic symbols do not have a unique compliance class, notational symbols do. A line in a painting is relatively replete as opposed to an electrocardiogram, which is attenuated, insofar as certain properties (thickness, tonality, or intensity) are relevant for the painting's symbolization but not for that of an electrocardiogram. Lastly, exemplification as well as multiple and complex reference are modes of symbolization commonly present in aesthetic symbols: while a word in a scientific text denotes univocally, the same word in a literary text may exemplify certain of its phonetic properties and refer to multiple things in a complex way.

The symptoms of the aesthetic function similarly to pathological symptoms: the latter point to a certain disease, the former to aesthetic symbolization. Similar to pathological symptoms, just as the presence of many symptoms does not imply that the disease is graver, the presence of most of the symptoms of the aesthetic does not imply that the symbol is more aesthetic; the presence of only one symptom does not mean that the symbol has a weak aesthetic functioning. The symptoms of the aesthetic are neither necessary nor sufficient conditions for aesthetic functioning, although they 'may be conjunctively sufficient and disjunctively necessary' (Goodman 1968: 254). While in the first formulation of the symptoms, Goodman maintained that it could be possible to have aesthetic functioning without the presence of any of the symptoms, he later stated that it is doubtful that there is aesthetic functioning without any of the symptoms being present (Goodman 1968: 254; Goodman 1984: 135–8), for it seems as though exemplification would always be present.

The symptoms are not ultimate criteria to establish what functions as an aesthetic symbol and what does not, but their presence suffices to indicate aesthetic functioning. 'When is architecture?' can then be answered resorting to the symptoms. Saltbox houses function as works of architecture when some of the symptoms are present: when referring to some of their properties as proportion, size, or materials, exemplification is present; when symbolizing a traditional construction, syntactic density and relative repleteness. On the other hand, when a saltbox house stands for an old building or a kind of building I like, none of the symptoms is present and thus it is not an architectural work. By looking for the presence or absence of symptoms, interpretation may be guided. It may seem that the symptoms constitute a weak criterion to identify works of architecture. But resorting to them suffices to distinguish aesthetic functioning in most of the cases and when not, other clues or indicators may be helpful, such as the context or what else is symbolized by the building. However tentative the symptoms may be, they are Goodman's only way to detect aesthetic functioning and they are conceptually necessary for his theory of symbols: if there was no way to distinguish between aesthetic and non-aesthetic symbolic functioning, there would be no way to explain why one and the same symbol functions in various ways.

The symptoms are not ultimate criteria to establish what functions as an aesthetic symbol and what does not, but their presence suffices to indicate aesthetic functioning.

CHAPTER 4

Identity of Architectural Works

Not all buildings have the same stature. While we distinguish between the Parthenon in Athens and the one in Nashville – one is the original and the other its copy – we consider that the constructions in a tract housing area are the same. The Parthenon in Nashville is an exact reproduction of the one in Athens, and a tract house is identical to the ones in its surroundings. The tract house, however, is not regarded as a copy, but as an instance of the same work. Similar issues rise with restored and reconstructed buildings. Since its construction in 1889, several parts of the Eiffel Tower have been replaced by new ones, so that there are less and less original construction materials, and yet the Eiffel Tower is regarded as the same. The 1986 reconstruction of the Barcelona Pavilion is considered the same as the 1929 Pavilion designed by Mies van der Rohe, but at the same time we also distinguish between 1929 and 1986 structures. These cases illustrate that there are different criteria to determine what constitutes the identity of a building and that there is not always a clear-cut distinction among them. Goodman was the first to undertake a systematic approach and provide decisive categories to philosophically discern between an original work and its copy, reproduction, or forgery. In *Languages of Art*, he devotes central chapters to deal with this issue, pointing out that different criteria are required when establishing authenticity in the various artistic disciplines. However clear these distinctions might be in cases such as painting or music, difficulties arise when dealing with architecture. To examine the specificities that architecture presents one has to consider first Goodman's account of identity and authenticity in general and also in relation to other arts.

Autographic and allographic

When discussing the characteristics of an original work, Goodman notes that some works of art cannot be faked. Whereas it is possible to have a perfect copy of a painting, no forgery of a known musical piece can be made. This leads him to distinguish between autographic as opposed to allographic arts, i.e., arts such as painting, which are 'fakable', and arts such as music, which he affirms are 'unfakable'. In his words:

> Let us speak of a work of art as *autographic* if and only if the distinction between original and forgery of it is significant; or better, if and only if even the most exact duplication of it does not thereby count as genuine. If a work of art is autographic, we may also call that art autographic. Thus painting is autographic, music nonautographic, or *allographic*.
>
> (Goodman 1968: 113, his emphasis)

The autographic identifies a category of works that cannot be replicated, i.e., every difference between a work and even its closest copy makes a difference to the work's identity. In contrast, the allographic identifies a category of works that can be replicated, i.e., the difference between an original and its duplication is irrelevant to the work's identity. This distinction implies two different criteria for establishing the identity of a work of art or architecture. In the autographic arts, authenticity is defined by the history of production: two works that do not share the same history of production are not considered the same work and hence one is the original and the other is something else, be it a copy, a reproduction, or a forgery. But if both works have in common the same history of production, then they are instances of the same work. The autographic does not entail singularity, for there are autographic and multiple works, such as engravings and cast sculptures. An artistic discipline is thus autographic if the identification of the works in this discipline necessarily depends on the history of production and this is not related to singularity or multiplicity.

On the other hand, the identity of allographic works is established by means of a notation: two literary texts are instances of a particular work if they are spelled exactly the same, and two musical pieces are instances of the same work if they comply with the same score. This implies that allographic works are potentially multiple and reproducible; there can be several instances of the same allographic work. Although these works of art also have histories of production, this is not the criterion for defining the work as it is. It is known, for example, that J. S. Bach composed the *Goldberg Variations* around 1741 for Count von Keyserling, who suffered from insomnia and wanted his harpsichordist J. G. Goldberg to play during his sleepless nights. Yet this is not the criterion followed to identify a musical piece as a performance of the *Goldberg Variations*; instead of the history of production of the piece, the criterion used is a notation, in this case a score. As Goodman affirms:

> Authority for a notation must be found in an antecedent classification by history of production; but definitive identification of works, fully freed from history of production, is achieved only when a notation is established. The allographic art has won its emancipation not by proclamation but by notation.
>
> (Goodman 1968: 122)

Despite having a history of production, music, literature, and performing arts are generally allographic, for a score, a text, or a script are needed to identify a work as such. There are, however, some exceptions: music with no score, such as jazz improvisations, is autographic. This shows that the categories of the autographic and the allographic are descriptive rather than prescriptive. Goodman observes how we traditionally identify works of art and proposes these notions to explain this process, but this does not imply the imposition of an unbreakable rule: insofar as artistic production evolves, the criteria to identify works may evolve as well. At present, painting, etching, and sculpture are usually autographic and music, literature, and the performing arts are usually allographic. Architecture, according to Goodman, can be classified under both categories:

> We are not as comfortable about identifying an architectural work with a design rather than a building as we are about identifying a musical work with a composition rather than a performance. In that architecture has a reasonably appropriate notational system and that some of its works are unmistakably allographic, the art is allographic. But insofar as its notational

> **language has not yet acquired full authority to divorce identity of work in all cases from particular production, architecture is a mixed and transitional case.**
>
> **(Goodman 1968: 221)**

Architecture is both autographic and allographic, given that both criteria for establishing the identity of a work are valid. Some buildings are identified by the history of their production, such as the Parthenon in Athens, while others by means of a notation, such as the several instances of tract housing. Moreover, a single building can be judged according to both criteria at the same time, because the first stage of the design can be considered allographic (determined by plans) and the second one as autographic (determined by the history of construction). This in-between position of architecture is not only synchronic, but also diachronic: defining architecture as a 'mixed case' means that the autographic and the allographic criteria coexist simultaneously, i.e., synchronic; defining it as a 'transitional case' means that the allographic criterion to establish the identity of an architectural work succeeds the autographic, i.e., diachronic, and thus presupposes an inherent historical process. This is precisely what Goodman assumes when he states that architecture will become completely allographic once its notational system has 'acquired full authority to divorce identity of work in all cases from particular production' (Goodman 1968: 221). Thus a decisive factor in determining whether architecture is autographic or allographic is the perfection of the correspondent notation, in this case, plans, elevations, sections, and details.

Architecture is both autographic and allographic, given that both criteria for establishing the identity of a work are valid.

Architecture's notation

Architectural plans – together with elevations, sections, and details – are developed in response to the need for participation of many hands in construction. They also have the logically prior function of establishing the identity of allographic works of architecture and, as such, they constitute architecture's notation. As seen in Chapter 3, notation is a kind of denotation with a very specific function in the arts, which is precisely the preservation of work-identity. Notations have to fulfil a series of strict requirements, because otherwise their purpose of identifying a work would not be achieved. When they fulfil these requirements, then they are what Goodman terms notational systems, as is the case of musical scores; when they partially fulfil them, they are notational schemes, as is the case of literary texts and drama scripts.

Comparing architectural plans with musical scores and drama scripts allows us to determine whether architecture's notation is a notational system or a notational scheme.

To preserve the identity of a musical work, a score has to correspond exactly to a performance and from that performance an exact replica of the initial score has to be derived. When the exact correspondence between score and performances is broken, these are no longer performances of the same musical piece. This entails that playing a single wrong note invalidates the performance as an instance of a work and hence only performances free of mistakes count as genuine. Although this is not the everyday understanding of what constitutes a musical performance, Goodman establishes this strict requirement because:

> The innocent-seeming principle that performances differing by just one note are instances of the same work risks the consequence [...] that all performances whatsoever are of the same work.

> (Goodman 1968: 186)

This requisite aims to avoid the so-called Sorites paradox, or little-by-little argument: imagine a heap of sand from which grains are removed one by one. Removing one grain does not make a difference in the heap, nor removing two, or three, but if we continue removing grains we are left with no heap. There is no way to tell at what amount of grains the heap ceases to be a heap, just as there is no way to determine how many wrong notes one can play before the performance ceases to be a genuine instance of a musical work. For this reason, scores and other notational systems have to fulfil this strict condition. A script, on the other hand, is a notational scheme because it only partially fulfils this correspondence. Whereas from a script one can derive a performance of a play, it is not possible to derive the exact script from the performance. When a character leaves the stage to the left and smiling, for example, there is no way to establish whether the stage directions were 'she leaves the stage', 'she leaves the stage to the left', or 'she leaves the stage to the left smiling'. An unavoidable degree of ambiguity is characteristic of notational schemes.

Comparing architectural plans with musical scores and drama scripts allows us to determine whether architecture's notation is a notational system or a notational scheme. Goodman's discussion in not helpful here, since he writes that plans can be both: notational systems and notational schemes. First:

> [A]lthough a drawing often counts as a sketch, and a measurement in numerals as a script, the particular selection of drawing and numerals in an architectural plan counts as a digital diagram and as a score.
>
> (Goodman 1968: 219)

Plans include integral parts that constitute a notation and others that do not. The notational parts result from the combination of accurate drawing and measurements represented on a scale, which would be parallel to the musical scale system; the non-notational parts are the written specifications or other non-codified indications regarding certain aspects of the building (such as construction materials), which would be comparable to the verbal specifications of tempo in a score. Despite these similarities, scores are much more codified than plans: while musical scores can resort to very precise codifications to establish how every single note has to be played ('·' for staccato, '-' for tenuto, or '>' for sforzando, to mention a few articulation signs in Western musical notation), architectural plans lack a similar system to fix how each and every one of their parts has to be executed. Therefore, extranotational information is (still) required to explicitly state constructive elements such as the wall texture or colour; these are usually exemplified by means of a sample: a piece of a wall with the correspondent definitive surface and colour serves as a model for the rest of the building. Yet there is another aspect that differentiates scores from plans and that points to the fact the plans resemble scripts. Given a certain plan (together with a specification book, which details the exact materials and equipment) it is possible to create an actual instance of the building, as long as the contractor knows how to interpret the information conveyed in plans. The converse, however, is not true; from a building it is not possible to derive a unique set of plans. This is the reason why Goodman provides a second characterization of plans:

> **An architect is free to stipulate that the material of a foundation be stone, or that it be granite, or that it be Rockport seam-faced granite. Given the building, we cannot tell which of these nesting terms occurs in the specifications. The class of buildings picked out by the plans-plus-specifications is narrower than that defined by the plans alone; but the plans-plus-specifications make up a script, not a score.**
>
> **(Goodman 1968: 219)**

Architecture's notation is hence a notational scheme that functions similarly to the drama's script, where there is no way to determine the precise stage directions that were given in the script. What is left to explore is whether it is feasible that plans develop into a perfect notational system to include the features now expressed in an extranotational way. This is a key issue for Goodman, because architecture will not become completely allographic until its notational system is able to completely fix the identity of architectural works. There has been an attempt to argue that 'Computer Aided Design' (CAD) theoretically allows the complete specification of the elements that are part of the architect's extranotational language by means of codification (Fisher 2000; see also Allen 2009). In this way, identification of architectural works could be independent of any particular building or, in other words, with the progressive transformation of plans from analogical to digital, plans would transform from notational schemes to notational systems and potentially become the only criterion to determine the identity of a building. Current practice, however, contradicts this assumption, as the next section shows.

Between autographic and allographic

Even though a perfect notational system could be available, some architectural works resist being considered only from an allographic perspective. As Goodman affirms:

> [A]ll houses complying with the plans for Smith-Jones Split-Level #17 are equally instances of that architectural work. But in the case of an earlier architectural tribute to womanhood, the Taj Mahal, we may bridle at considering another building from the same plans and even on the same site to be an instance of the same work rather than a copy.
>
> (Goodman 1968: 220–1)

Although it is possible to build a copy of the Taj Mahal, the criterion to identify this building is still the history of its construction and not a notation. Not knowing exactly every detail of its history of production does not invalidate the possibility of establishing the work's identity autographically. To identify the Taj Mahal, it suffices to know, for instance, that it was built between roughly 1631 and 1654, that it was designed by several people (although we do not know exactly what parts were under the supervision of which designer), and that around 20,000 people worked on its construction (although we do not know what every single one of them did or who they were). Even if we did not possess any information about the history of production of a work, this would not invalidate the autographic criterion of determining its identity. This is the case of anonymous buildings, such as most ancient temples and medieval cathedrals and churches, whose history of production is impossible to trace back and yet they can only be autographically identified. Hence, an antecedent classification of works as autographic or allographic is logically prior to the availability of a notation.

The above-mentioned passage also implies another aspect: the difference between multiple allographic buildings and singular autographic architectural works is sometimes related to the distinction between the so-called high and low architecture. While tract housing sprawls throughout suburban areas and this process has no effect on its identity, no masterpiece of architecture is reproduced without emphasizing that the subsequent instances are not the original but simply replicas (the Parthenon in Nashville is just a copy of the one in Athens). It thus seems that, for buildings aesthetically less valuable, the identity criterion is the allographic and, for the others, it is the autographic. This assessment need not be permanent, but may change depending on the development of architecture. In fact, in his Office of Metropolitan Architecture (OMA), Rem Koolhaas has created 'Generics', a department devoted to designing what Goodman might have called 'high quality allographic architecture'. OMA aims to design without patents, copyright, and signature, so that their projects can be universally shared (Graaf 2008); ironically, this allographic architecture has the imprint of an autographic architect. In addition to this, there exists a dichotomy between potential reproducibility and actual limitation in the construction of architectural works, which can be summarized as follows:

> The case of architecture may seem paradoxical, because this art, which today possesses systems of (de)notation powerful enough to make possible the indefinite multiplication of its realizations, never exploits this possibility, except in aesthetically least prestigious productions [...]. As to the unique character of works of high fashion (actually, I am told, one realization of each is authorized *per continent*, whatever that rather hazy geographical term may mean), it stems in part from a deliberate restriction whose motives are obvious, and in part from the autographic nature of this practice – for not only does nothing prevent an art from functioning in one regime in the case of certain of its works, and in the other in the case of certain others; it is also quite possible for one and the same work to be autographic in one of its parts and allographic in another.
>
> (Genette 1997: 97, his emphasis)

It thus seems that, for buildings aesthetically less valuable, the identity criterion is the allographic, and, for the others, it is the autographic.

Architecture has thus a double nature; it is a 'mixed and transitional case', not only because some buildings are considered autographic while at the same time others are taken to be allographic, but also because some of their parts are autographic and others allographic. This is the case of autographic buildings containing an allographic inscription, such as the various churches with the inscription 'me fecit' referring to who built them. Yet architecture can be considered partly autographic and partly allographic from another point of view. According to Goodman, arts can be classified into one-stage and two-stage arts (Goodman 1968: 114–15). Architecture is a two-stage art, because first it is necessary to design a building and then to actually build it, which implies two phases in the construction process. Precisely for this reason a notation was developed: to assure the correct transition from design to construction in a process in which several people intervene. Architecture can be considered allographic in its first phase and autographic in the second phase. The plan is allographic because its relevant aspect is to accurately reproduce a series of specifications that fix the identity of a building and, for this sake, the history of its production is irrelevant; it does not matter whether the plan itself is the first and original one (if existing). The actual building, which corresponds to the second phase, is autographic, for the history of production is the criterion necessary to distinguish between two buildings that follow the same plan, i.e., the first phase of an architectural work. This is the only way to distinguish, for example, between the Cinderella Castle built in 1971 in the Walt Disney Resort in Florida and the one built in 1983 for the Tokyo Disney Resort.

It may seem that the distinction between the two Cinderella Castles – and, in general, the distinction among identical works – is possible only if site-specificity is taken as a requisite of their histories of production. At first glance it may even seem that architecture is always site-specific. But this statement cannot be generalized, otherwise some buildings that have been moved would not be the same building any more: the Pergamon Altar now in the Pergamon Museum in Berlin would not be the Pergamon Altar, for it is not in Pergamon, but in Berlin. Moreover, the autographic criterion is still valid for distinguishing between two identical works located on different sites, even if the history of production does not necessarily entail site-specificity as one of its necessary elements: it is enough to know that there is one Cinderella Castle built in 1971 and another in 1983 to discriminate one from the other. And if both had been built at exactly the same time, different people would have participated in the construction and thus their histories of production would continue being different and valid as an identification criterion. Therefore, location is not an indispensable condition for a work to be autographic and, although some autographic works are site-specific (such as the Taj Mahal), this does not imply that all other autographic works, such as paintings, sculptures, and etchings, have to be site-specific.

Another kind of construction that illustrates the complexity of architecture's identity is that of restorations, architectural amalgams where the autographic and the allographic criteria collide. If architecture is only allographic, then a building is restored by following the notation and by repairing or reconstructing the missing or damaged elements of that building according to the features established in plans. Consider the Romanesque monastery of Sant Pere de Rodes, located in the north-east of Spain (Figure 11). This complex was mainly built during the tenth and eleventh centuries with some posterior additions built until 1798, when the monastery was definitively abandoned. After sporadic restorations undertaken in the 1930s, the main restoration work took place between 1989 and 1999, the result of which is the building now extant. Since, if allographic, its history of production is irrelevant, the restored building has to be taken as another instance of this allographic work – or better, the only instance.

Another kind of construction that illustrates the complexity of architecture's identity is that of restorations, architectural amalgams where the autographic and the allographic criteria collide.

Figure 11 Cloister of the Monastery of Sant Pere de Rodes.

There is one aspect, however, that obliges us to qualify this assessment, which is that the interventions undertaken to restore Sant Pere de Rodes are visible. In restoration terms, a purist, and not an integral, restoration was done. An integral restoration intends to repair a work to make the whole look original, whereas a purist or archaeological restoration contends that any substitution or addition has to be visible to avoid any pretence of authenticity. In this latter case, the missing parts are not replaced with pieces indistinguishable from the already existing ones, but clearly discernible from the old ones. The missing arches, columns, and capitals from the Monastery's cloister, for instance, were built using concrete cement, explicitly showing that they were prostheses to an original work (Figure 11). This means that Sant Pere de Rodes is not simply considered as an allographic work, for the distinction between its original and its newer parts is relevant and, consequently, the monastery is also autographic.

If architecture is considered as only autographic, then a restoration can be regarded as an alteration of the building, since it implies replacing, adding, and also eliminating some traces of the history of production of the building. These traces could also disappear through the effect of aging, and the autographic criterion would nonetheless remain valid for determining the identity of the work. Although a restored building would not wholly be like the initial building, it is still the same building as long as the original can be identified as such by the same history of production (Elgin 1997a: 106). Yet it is not clear if we could still consider Sant Pere de Rodes the same building if, for preservation's sake, each and every one of the original pieces were replaced with new ones. This is similar to the logical paradox of the ship of Theseus, whose planks were gradually substituted for new ones when they became damaged at sea until there was no trace left of the original ship and thus posing the question whether or not it was the same ship that returned ashore. As a corollary, one can question what happens if the replaced planks were used to build a second ship. If the stones that constituted the monastery were used to build the exact building, we could ask which of the monasteries, if any, is the original work. If allographic, then both buildings would be instances of the same work. If autographic, then it would be first necessary to determine which elements of the history of production of both buildings are relevant to the work's identity: if the materials make the work to be the original, then only the second monastery would be the original; if place is relevant, then the complete reconstructed building would be the original. Certainly, as Goodman himself affirms,

> **not every art can be classed as autographic or as allographic. This classification applies only where we have some means of sorting objects or events into works – that is, where there is some criterion for identity of a work.**
>
> **(Goodman 1984: 139)**

Yet architecture can indeed be classified according to these two categories, as the several examples discussed in this chapter illustrate. Moreover, through the autographic and the allographic we can conceptually differentiate between an original and a copy, a reproduction, or even a forgery. The difficulties that arise when establishing what constitutes an architectural work are nothing less than a reflection of the complexities inherent in architecture itself when it comes to issues of identity; these are clearly illustrated in the case of the Barcelona Pavilion.

Autographic versus allographic: the Barcelona Pavilion

Mies van der Rohe's German Pavilion (now known as Barcelona Pavilion) was originally designed as a temporary structure for the 1929 International Exposition in Barcelona and rebuilt in 1986 as a permanent building (Figure 12). One can consider that the 1986 pavilion is a copy – hence autographic; that the two pavilions are instances of the same work – hence allographic; or that they are two different buildings – autographic again; but neither of them completely defines the pavilion's identity status. Rather, it is characterized by continuous shift between the autographic and the allographic, which reflects Goodman's assertion that architecture is a mixture of both.

The main argument for rebuilding the 1929 pavilion was its stature as a unique work of modern architecture. Being a unique work entails considering that the Barcelona Pavilion is autographic and, hence, that the 1986 pavilion is a replica

Figure 12 Reconstructed Barcelona Pavilion, Barcelona.

of the 1929 one. The history of production is significant and what allows us to distinguish between the original and its replica: one has a history of construction that took place under certain conditions in the spring of 1929 and the other has a history of construction under other conditions that took place between 1983 and 1986. Accordingly, the Barcelona Pavilion is an autographic work of architecture: we distinguish and consider that the difference between original and replica is relevant. This could seem the general view, particularly because the 1986 building is defined as a reconstruction, and not as the original. Yet this is not conclusive enough for determining the identities of the 1929 and the 1986 pavilions and incontestably assuming that they are two different buildings. When the reconstructed pavilion was dedicated, Mies van der Rohe's daughter affirmed that 'for a second time, the German Pavilion of Barcelona has been given to the world' (Amela 1986: 52). Only a work that is not unique can be given 'for a second time' and still continue to be the same; only allographic works can be reproduced and maintain the same identity, which compels us to affirm that the building recovered in 1986 is the same as the one erected in 1929. Here the autographic distinction between original and replica is meaningless, because a unique and original work – a work of which there is only one – cannot be given twice. Only if allographic can there be the pavilion for a second time. This is the first oscillation between autographic and allographic criteria, which is continuous throughout the process of reconstruction, and shows how autographic and allographic features are inextricably interwoven when determining the identity of the Barcelona Pavilion.

Although the autographic character of the pavilion is what allows us to distinguish between the two buildings, to build the 1986 pavilion the criterion followed was not the history of production of the building, but the recreation of plans.

The most important obstacle confronted in reconstructing Mies' Pavilion was the absence of reliable and definitive plans, as the originals were lost (Solà-Morales *et al.* 1993: 9). Thus the first step was to fix its identity by means of a notation, i.e., new plans, sections, and elevations. Although the autographic character of the pavilion is what allows us to distinguish between the two buildings, to build the 1986 pavilion the criterion followed was not the history of production of the building, but the recreation of plans. Besides, it is literally impossible to reproduce the history of production of the 1929 pavilion to build the 1986 one and, therefore, the only way to rebuild the pavilion is by developing a series of plans. The identity of the Barcelona Pavilion is thus established by allographic processes. As Goodman says:

> [W]hile availability of a notation is usually what establishes an art as allographic, mere availability of a notation is neither a necessary nor a sufficient condition. What is *necessary* is that identification of the or an instance of a work be independent of the history of production; a notation as much codifies as creates such an independent criterion.
>
> (Goodman 1984: 139, his emphasis)

This is precisely the case of the Barcelona Pavilion. Despite lacking a notation that uniquely determined the work, it was possible to identify the work without relying on the history of its construction. Thus the pavilion is here rather allographic than autographic, because it is actually possible to create a notation and because the history of its construction is not decisive to fix its identity. Nevertheless, the process of allographically establishing the identity of the pavilion was open-ended: there was no way to fix 'beyond all doubt' its identity, for not all the available sources provided the same information, thus they could not be relied on (Solà-Morales *et al.* 1993: 5). One could think that such uncertainty invalidates the possibility of establishing the identity of Mies' work in an allographic way. That it is not possible to exactly determine each and every one of the features that constituted the 1929 building does not mean, however, that we cannot establish its identity by means of a notation, given that some of the properties are irrelevant when establishing identity. Parallel cases in other arts reveal that uncertainty is not an impediment to defining an architectural work by means of a plan: critical editions of literary works compare several versions of the same work and, in case of conflict, one of them (or a specific passage) is established as the canonical one. Much the same occurs when there are several versions of a musical score and the identity of the piece is established by fixing a unique score. Hence new plans, elevations for each façade, and various sections and details of the pavilion were developed, specifying several features that had not been defined in previous plans, and thus fixing what would constitute its identity in an unprecedented way. From that moment, following Goodman, only the building that fulfils the conditions established by these notations can be considered the Barcelona Pavilion. The main reconstruction criterion for the 1986 pavilion is key at this point:

> [A]n undisputed premise here was the concept of a reconstruction that would interpret as faithfully as possible the idea and the material form of the 1929 Pavilion. If we have made a distinction between idea and material form, it is because the study of the materials used in the project, alongside other contemporary schemes by its architect, indicates that the physical execution of the building, for reasons of economy, haste or simple

technological limitations, did not always come up to the level of its ideal character before, during and after construction.

(Solà-Morales *et al.* 1993: 29)

Here Goodman's terms prompt us to consider that the pavilion is allographic; the 'ideal character' of the work would correspond to a work whose features are completely established by a notation, and the 'material form' would be an actual built instance of this work. Yet, according to this premise, the 1929 pavilion would not be a perfect version of the Barcelona Pavilion: it is known that due to the scarcity of green marble and travertine, some walls were made out of brick and painted green and yellow (Solà-Morales *et al.* 1993: 14). The built 1929 pavilion was only an approximation of what it actually should have been: a building that apparently was the Barcelona Pavilion, but did not possess some of its defining properties. This would bring us to the perplexing conclusion that the pavilion built in 1929 is not the actual Barcelona Pavilion, and that the 1986 building is indeed an instance of the pavilion – the first and only instance of the pavilion, because it accurately fulfils the requirements established by the plans.

Our intuitive reluctance to conclude that the 1929 pavilion is not the Barcelona Pavilion points to the need to shift the identity criterion again, from allographic to autographic, and recognize that the pavilion's identity is not totally defined by a plan. While scores and scripts seem to be sufficient in fixing the identity of musical pieces and plays and the differences among instances do not matter for establishing their identity, this seems not to be the case for architectural plans, since extranotational information (referring to the construction materials, for example) is required to absolutely determine a building. Two reasons may explain why this extra information is necessary: because the notation of architecture is not accurate enough to completely establish identity; or because some features that constitute a building's identity cannot be allographically fixed, i.e., even with a perfect notation, the autographic criterion is still pertinent. This is exactly the case of the Barcelona Pavilion: on the one hand, we can only distinguish between original and replica through the different histories of constructions – autographically; and, on the other, the reconstruction was only possible by means of a notation – allographically. The pavilion is thus a mix of autographic and allographic, and precisely this hybrid status allows us to understand some aspects that otherwise we could not understand, such as the difference between original and replica and, simultaneously, the possibility of a replica.

Our intuitive reluctance to conclude that the 1929 pavilion is not the Barcelona Pavilion points to the need to shift the identity criterion again, from allographic to autographic, and recognize that the pavilion's identity is not totally defined by a plan.

This brings us to clarify Goodman's initial assertion that notations are what grant emancipation to allographic arts. While it is true that precise and accurate notations are required, it is also necessary that the difference between two architectural works based on the same plan be irrelevant. Goodman's further assessment that architecture is a 'mixed and transitional' case and that will become completely allographic once its notation is perfected needs to be revised also. Architecture is certainly a mixed case, but it is uncertain that it is transitional, because the achievement of a notation that completely identifies a work does not necessarily entail that its identity will be independent from its history of production. In other words, it is uncertain whether autographic features will ever cease being constitutive to the work's identity, which precludes us to state that architecture is a transitional case; but this does not exclude the possibility that sometime in the future the allographic criterion will be enough for identifying architectural works. The pertinence of the identity criteria goes hand by hand with the transformations in architecture and thus they may become useless if the features that characterize architectural works as such change. At present, the autographic and the allographic help us in clarifying and classifying our judgements regarding the identity of a work; they are a reflection of our practice of distinguishing the constitutive elements of a work as well as of discriminating between an original, a reproduction, and a forgery.

Goodman's categories of the autographic and the allographic allow us to establish the identity of an architectural work. There are some works that are clearly autographic (the Taj Mahal), other clearly allographic (tract housing), and yet other buildings that are considered from both the autographic and the allographic perspectives (as copies and restorations show). Thus, not only is architecture a hybrid because it simultaneously comprises autographic as well as allographic works, but these two criteria are also intertwined within one and the same building. Both identity criteria are interlaced insofar as the first stage of the construction process of a building is allographic and the second stage autographic. Both criteria are inextricably linked insofar as the two are necessary to identify one and the same building: the autographic criterion serves to distinguish two identical buildings (such as the two Cinderella Castles) and, at the same time, the allographic criterion allows us to actually build two identical buildings (such as the Cinderella Castle in Orlando and the one in Tokyo). This array of possibilities does not have to be interpreted as a failure in the process of identifying works, but as evidence of the inherent complexity and richness of architecture. Goodman's affirmation that architecture is a hybrid case is a reflection of the way in which we judge the buildings' identity. On the one hand, some buildings are judged according to their history of production; on the other, some buildings are judged taking a notation as the criterion; and sometimes both criteria are used for one and the same building. The cause of this mixture lies not only in the lack of a perfect notation to identify works, but in our current reluctance to judge some buildings exclusively from an allographic or an autographic perspective (as the Barcelona Pavilion shows). Given that architecture is continually evolving, what constitutes a building's identity and what criterion applies needs to be permanently assessed (as OMA's 'Generics' case illustrates).

Goodman's affirmation that architecture is a hybrid case is a reflection of the way in which we judge the buildings' identity.

CHAPTER 5

Buildings as Ways of Worldmaking

[W]e do not make stars as we make bricks; not all making is a matter of molding mud. The worldmaking mainly in question here is making not with hands but with minds, or rather with languages or other symbol systems.

(Goodman 1984: 42)

So far symbols, symbol systems, and the various modes of reference have been discussed stressing their role of enabling, conveying, and creating meanings. This is the epistemological side of Goodman's constructive relativism, according to which there is a plurality of equally right interpretations of any given symbol that provide a multiplicity of meanings. Its metaphysical counterpart entails that this plurality of equally right interpretations corresponds to a plurality of worlds or world-versions. Architects contribute to the process of worldmaking not simply in the physical sense of making bricks, but most importantly in a metaphysical one, by creating symbols and symbol systems that further constitute worlds. This chapter discusses the transition from epistemology to metaphysics, Goodman's conception of a plurality of worlds or world-versions, the several processes of worldmaking, and examines how architecture can uniquely contribute to the making and remaking of worlds.

From epistemology to metaphysics: worldmaking

Symbols are characterized by the fact that they bear multiple interpretations and can convey several meanings. From another point of view, the same meaning can be symbolized in various ways within different symbol systems. The same harmonic proportion can be symbolized by architecture, music, and mathematics. Some of the rooms at Palladio's Villa Rotonda, for instance, symbolize harmonic proportions, which can be mathematically represented as 1:1, 2:1, and 3:4. The ground floor is a square that corresponds to a 1:1

proportion, the rectangular rooms at each corner follow a 2:1 proportion (two double squares) and, adjacent to them, there are smaller rectangular rooms that correspond to a proportion of 3:4 (a square plus its third). Some musical intervals also correspond to these proportions: a unison sounds when two strings of the same length vibrate (1:1), two strings in which one is twice as long as the other produce an octave (2:1), and a perfect fourth (the chord of C and F, for instance) sounds when the relationship between two strings is 3:4. These three different ways of symbolizing provide a unique understanding of harmonic proportion. Architecture conveys a spatial comprehension of proportion, music an acoustic one, and math an arithmetical one; by comparing these ways, new insights on harmonic proportion may arise. For Goodman, none of these three ways is categorically better than the other ones, i.e., there is no hierarchy among the several systems, but rather they are equally valid in conveying meaning. Moreover, the meaning provided by each symbol system is not completely translatable to any other one, so their ways of understanding are not interchangeable: proportion as symbolized by a musical interval can certainly be verbally described or represented by a mathematical formula, but the proportional duration symbolized in music gets lost in the transposition to another system. There is thus a plurality of symbol systems irreducible to one another and it is not possible to reduce all of them to a shared system that would serve as common ground for equalizing the various kinds of understanding:

> So long as contrasting right versions not all reducible to one are countenanced, unity is to be sought not in an ambivalent or neutral *something* beneath these versions but in an overall organization embracing them.
>
> (Goodman 1976: 5, his emphasis)

the meaning provided by each symbol system is not completely translatable to any other one, so their ways of understanding are not interchangeable

Therefore, reality is not fixed and immutable, but constructed. There is not a ready-made world from which unchangeable facts are extracted: worlds and its components are made. And any discipline that contributes to the advancement of understanding through symbol systems, such as architecture contributes also to the creation of a world: the ways of creating meaning are also, in Goodman's terminology, ways of worldmaking.

The overall organization is the one provided by symbols and symbol systems. That there is no 'neutral *something*' means that there is not 'a' world or 'the' world to provide unity, but only a plurality of symbol systems. These systems are also worlds or versions, because they are what actually constitute the world, and this is how creating meaning and making worlds, symbolization and construction, epistemology and metaphysics are inextricably linked. Since there is a plurality of systems that may create incompatible worlds, there is not only one way in which things really are. Light, for instance, can either be understood as a wave or as a particle, and these two interpretations, based on two different symbol systems, actually create two different worlds with different criteria of rightness. These worlds are irreducible to one another; there is no world where light is a wave and a particle simultaneously. Likewise, the heliocentric and the geocentric systems constitute two different worlds, not 'different versions of the "same facts"' (Goodman 1978: 93), and it is not the case that one is absolutely true and the other absolutely false, but rather that each version has its own criteria. 'The sun rises in the east' only makes sense and is true in a geocentric world-version, which is the one we commonly live in. Therefore, reality is not fixed and immutable, but constructed. There is not a ready-made world from which unchangeable facts are extracted: worlds and its components are made. And any discipline that contributes to the advancement of understanding through symbol systems, such as architecture, contributes also to the creation of a world: the ways of creating meaning are also, in Goodman's terminology, ways of worldmaking.

Note, however, that it is not possible to create from nothing: to make a world is always and only to remake it. For this reason Goodman talks indistinctively of both worlds and world-versions, because a world is always a modification or version of another one:

Worldmaking begins with one version and ends with another.

(Goodman 1978: 97)

Worldmaking is similar to language in that a new language is not created from nothing, but from an already existing one. We can introduce new words to designate new insights, but this creation takes place within a language. Or, more generally, worldmaking does not start from zero or from a given immutable world in the same way in which we do not start understanding things from scratch, but from a series of previous beliefs and conceptions. Also, worldmaking is a never-ending and open-ended process, for a version or an interpretation of the world is always susceptible of being modified: its symbolic functioning can reorganize, point out, or bring to the background the constitutive elements of a version without ever reaching an ultimate world and without knowing what the next world will look like. Since construing a world is always and also constructing a world, the criteria to consider that a world is right are the same as the ones that serve to consider that an interpretation is right. It is not the case that anything goes, but the criteria of rightness, adequacy, coherency, and consistency that determine what interpretations are acceptable are also valid for world-versions.

There are many ways of worldmaking. Goodman comments on several, such as composition, decomposition, weighting, ordering, deletion, supplementation, and deformation (Goodman 1978: 7–17). This list, however, is not conclusive. Worlds can be created by combining them and also by other processes, which in their turn can also be combined. Irony, variation, and quotation are ways of worldmaking common in the arts, for example. Even though these last three ways are also modes of reference, this does not mean that there is a direct correspondence between modes of reference (denotation, exemplification, expression, and so on) and ways of worldmaking. Rather, through symbolization, 'processes involved in building a world out of others' take place, that is, 'processes that go into worldmaking' occur (Goodman 1978: 7). Likewise, rather than saying that architecture is a way of worldmaking, it should be stated that architectural works and the several interpretations they bear as symbols contribute to the advancement of understanding and, therefore, to the creation of worlds. Or, in other words, architecture resorts to the several ways of worldmaking to make and remake the world.

Architectural ways of worldmaking

Architecture can offer new insights in a way that no other discipline can provide and, in so doing, create unique versions of the world that, in their turn, can influence or contribute to other versions. By symbolizing in several different ways, architecture can mould or reshape our perception and reorganize our understanding of the worlds or world-versions that constitute reality. To examine architecture's symbolic functioning entails examining the processes through which meanings are created and conveyed and, since symbolization is involved in worldmaking processes, this helps also to better understand how a particular world-version is made or remade. Without being exhaustive, the examples below (most of them already discussed in previous chapters) aim to illustrate how architecture may contribute to the making and remaking of worlds and world-versions.

Architecture can offer new insights in a way that no other

discipline can provide and, in so doing, create unique versions

of the world that, in their turn, can influence or contribute

to other versions. By symbolizing in several different ways, architecture can mould or reshape our perception and reorganize our understanding of the worlds or world-versions that constitute reality.

Consider the Sydney Opera House as a case of denotation in architecture. This building represents a group of sails if the building's shape is interpreted as corresponding to sails in the wind, but it can also represent shells, Albert Einstein's white messy hair, or Son Goku's hair when he adopts the super saiyan form. When interpreting the Sydney Opera House in these ways, the building is inserted into different symbol systems and, hence, also in different world-versions. Furthermore, another process takes place: worlds that were separated are now put in contact through this multiple denotation and, through this, new insights and versions may arise. That the Sydney Opera House denotes both Einstein's and Son Goku's hair can bring us to understand Einstein as a super warrior of physics, and perhaps we can further consider that Einstein's accomplishments are as extraordinary as Son Goku's powers and abilities. The world of physics and the world of manga are linked together through the symbolization in this building; through worldmaking processes like complementation and weighting another version is created. One could think that this superimposition of fictional and non-fictional versions, of the world of physics and the world of manga, is an exception. This is not so. Inasmuch as a symbol can denote fictively and not fictively at the same time, overlapping occurs. In other words, one and the same symbol can be an 'x-denotation' or a 'denotation of': the Sydney Opera House is a 'Son Goku's hair-denotation' and not a 'denotation of Son Goku's hair', because there is no such thing as Son Goku's hair; it is both a 'Einstein's hair-denotation' and a 'denotation of Einstein's hair' as well as a 'sails-denotation' and a 'denotation of sails', because there are such things as hair and sails. Since a building can have null denotation or refer to something, fictional and non-fictional worlds can potentially converge in architecture and create or remake world-versions.

There are also buildings with null denotation that contribute to the making of a fictional world, as happens with the Cinderella and Sleeping Beauty Castles in the Disney resorts as well as with Juliet's House in Verona. These are 'x-representations' and not 'representations of', in the same way as Grimm's and Shakespeare's descriptions of these buildings and the several representations through paintings, drawings, opera and ballet stage sets, and even toys are 'x-representations' and not 'representations of'. Architecture's particular contribution in this specific context is that it provides a very high degree of realism to a fictional version so that it can even be mistaken with non-fictional world-versions, something that usually does not happen with other fictional representations. Buildings that represent fictionally look exactly like buildings that do not represent anything and, in addition to their symbolic function, they may also carry out practical functions. By providing an actual space to an imaginary story, by supplementing a world-version with a realist framework, these buildings contribute to the confusion between fiction and non-fiction. Juliet's House is part of the fictional Verona created by Shakespeare, a version that now physically overlaps with the actual city. Buildings with null denotation contribute to the creation of fictional world-versions with the same characteristics of non-fictional ones, thus creating a superimposition or even a fusion of versions.

The previous examples dealt with buildings with null denotation that create a unique relay between everyday and fictional worlds. This is not to say that architecture's only role is to turn fictions into amusement parks and to allow fictional worlds to be inhabited. Precisely architecture's potential to provide three-dimensional versions is what allows the realization of other sorts of imaginary worlds that can be inhabited and can make a difference in people's lives. Many architectural projects are prompted by political imaginaries that aim to change and improve our everyday world; Ernst May's projects, for example, put into praxis the political imaginary of socialism through his buildings and designs. In Goodman's terms, through architecture an imaginary world-version reconfigures and introduces new elements to an existing world. The superimposition of actual worlds with imaginary ones does not necessarily entail deception, but rather opens up the process of worldmaking and creativity, not only from an artistic, but also from a social, political, and even revolutionary perspective.

Precisely architecture's potential to provide three-dimensional versions is what allows the realization of other sorts of imaginary worlds that can be inhabited and can make a difference in people's lives.

Copies and reproductions of buildings represent another building in its entirety. It could thus seem that copies constitute or are part of a duplication of the world-version to which the original belongs. The Eiffel Tower in Las Vegas would then be part of a duplicate version of the world that contains the Eiffel Tower in Paris. Despite some common features, copies do not symbolize the same things as the buildings they represent nor do they symbolize in the same way, and hence no exact duplication of a version takes place. Whereas both the Eiffel Tower in Paris and the one in Las Vegas symbolize France, only the first one symbolizes the centennial of the French Revolution, thus becoming a symbol for France's national values and being part, so to speak, of a political and national world-version. The tower in Las Vegas also stands for Paris as the city of love – its aim is to provide a place to recreate a romantic experience one may have in Paris, and in that way it may be part of another sort of version, perhaps even a kitsch version. Hence, copies and reproductions do not produce an exact duplicate of a certain world-version, but rather, through deformation, ponderation, irony, or exaggeration, another version, based upon the version to which the original belongs, is created. Versions that entail copies or reproductions do not necessarily have to share the same character as the version they are copies of.

A case related to that of copies and reproductions is the one of restoration, preservation, and reconstruction of buildings. The purpose of historic preservation is to partially or totally recover buildings that are relevant due to historic, social, cultural, or aesthetic reasons (Stubbs 2009). This does not only entail alterations to the building's structure and materials, but its symbolic functioning can also be modified in various degrees, which consequently entails that the building's contribution to the making of a world-version may also vary. The less invasive of the interventions is the cleaning and maintenance of buildings, which restores the building's initial appearance and through this its symbolic functioning is preserved (Elgin 1997a: 97–109). When a building is so dirty that the characteristics of the material do not come through, they cannot be symbolized; a proper cleaning can bring them to light again and recuperate a world-version. Nevertheless, restoring the past in a pristine way may sometimes be inadequate, because cleaning can also eliminate certain features, alter the symbolization, and thus eliminate some elements that constitute or influence a world-version, as would happen if one would bring green copper roofs to their original metallic colour. Some conservation solutions can achieve the cleaning and preservation of the previous 'dirty' state and in that way also preserve two world-versions, or at least the access to a world-version that is no longer there. This is precisely what happens in New York's Grand Central Station, whose main ceiling was restored to unveil the celestial sphere hidden behind layers of black dirt caused by tar from tobacco smoke. The entire ceiling was cleaned except for a small patch of grime at a corner, a remainder of the ceiling's previous state. By keeping this, both original and temporary appearance, their symbolic functioning and interpretations, as well as their corresponding world-versions were preserved by superimposition.

In visible interventions, the so-called purist or archaeological restorations, generally a superimposition and complementation of world-versions occurs. The building can be perceived as a whole, but given that the added elements are clearly distinguishable from the original ones, there is an unambiguous demarcation between original and reconstruction: symbolization and versions from two or more different periods are noticeable. In non-visible, so-called integral restorations, the intervention is unnoticeable and there is no perceptible difference among original and intervention, two options are possible. It may be an honest restoration, and then its outcomes are similar to those of cleaning and a world-version is recuperated, as happens with the Guggenheim Museum in New York. Or it may be an inventive restoration, and then the result is not the previous version, but rather a remade and reinterpreted world, as is the case of most of Viollet-le-Duc's projects such as his intervention in Notre-Dame in Paris, which are nineteenth-century versions of medieval structures. As a recreated version that pretends to faithfully recuperate the past, there is the possibility of deception: medieval and nineteenth-century versions are fused to each other and they are almost indistinguishable to an untrained eye. Here the restoration process deforms a version and creates another one by mixing elements from different times. Something similar may happen with reconstructions of no longer extant buildings: Mies van der Rohe's Barcelona Pavilion pretends to be a faithful reproduction of the original structure built in 1929, but some aspects of the reconstruction – the lack of the black carpet which together with the red curtain and the onyx wall created the German flag in the 1929 pavilion – cause the reconstructed pavilion to cease being a symbol for the German nation, as was the original. Now, the pavilion is rather an icon of modern architecture and is part of a world-version different from the initial one. This may entail confusion, since the reproduction pretends to be exactly as the original when it is rather a built interpretation. If it is not taken into account that the reconstruction is a revision of the original building, the process of making and remaking versions can be altered and limited by this. As with copies, one cannot assume that preservation achieves an exact recreation of a certain world-version, but that deformation, superimposition, ponderation, and even falsification of previous world-versions is possible.

one cannot assume that preservation achieves an exact recreation of a certain world-version

Since exemplification is one of the most frequent ways in which architecture symbolizes and a building can potentially exemplify any of its properties, it is also the mode by which buildings can contribute most to worldmaking. All the examples discussed in Chapter 3 can be now understood as ways of contributing to the making and remaking of worlds in a more or less subtle manner. By modelling space, light, and construction materials, buildings can create environments that can make us aware of previously unnoticed features. The central nave of some Renaissance churches create a perspectival, regular, and uniform space that, once experienced, may enable us to see the space outside the church in a perspectival centred way. On the other hand, Baroque churches create dynamic spaces and in motion that, once experienced, can bring us to perceive space in a different way than the Renaissance churches. These two conceptions of space (perspectival and dynamic) form two different world-versions, a Renaissance and a Baroque one. The relationship between these two can be understood as one of remaking a version, thus showing that worldmaking begins with other versions: by suppressing or relegating to the background some aspects of Renaissance space such as regularity, perspective, or closure, and bringing to light dynamism and sinuosity, a Baroque version emerges. By exemplifying properties such as forms, structure, construction elements, materials, or function in a distinct way, architecture contributes to enhance, nuance, or shift their meanings. The Villa Rotonda's exemplification of proportion and symmetry, the exemplification of rhythm at the Maison du Brésil, or the successive exemplifications of transparency, translucency, and opacity of the glass at Harvard's Science Center, all contribute and enrich the world-versions they are part of.

Buildings that express may also contribute to the creation of a world-version. The Jewish Museum in Berlin architecturally expresses a series of features that contribute to understanding the Holocaust and crucial events of history and, through them, this building participates to the weighing, enhancement, and complementation of a world-version. Not only the Jewish Museum, but many other elements, such as the memory of the survivors, documents, documentaries, literary and artistic works, or history, also make up this world. The museum's specific contribution to that version is that it expresses feelings, emotions, and unique events that visitors can aesthetically experience, and not just conceptually grasp, thus gaining a unique comprehension of this world and also about themselves that further remakes a world-version that lacked these elements. The unsettlement experienced at the Garden of Exile, for example, enhances the conception of exile with a physical awkwardness and discomfort and complements this world-version in a way that no other discipline does.

Similarly, buildings symbolizing in complex and multiple ways can complement, reshape, and establish a relation between world-versions that were previously not in contact. Through allusion, buildings can create a superimposition of different world-versions. All the world-versions to which the buildings that allude to the Pantheon in Rome belong (the Villa Rotonda, the Pantheon in Paris, Jefferson's Rotunda, or Low Memorial Library) are connected through this symbolization and this may result in mutual influences among worlds. The allusions to different styles in the Vanna Venturi House create a clash among world-versions and, as irony comes into play, a new version that deforms some aspects and emphasizes other elements of the previous ones emerges. By ironically referring to the strict separation between architectural styles through their combination in the same building, the Vanna Venturi House challenges the traditional separation among styles and melds them all in a version. Variations can contribute to the creation of a world-version complementing and reordering elements of previous versions into a new one, and style can do so similarly by grouping under the same category elements that otherwise seemed not to be related at all. The progressive modifications of the Latin cross plan may bring some details and their meanings from one version to another; the works by architects that seemed to have few features in common were assembled under the so-called deconstructivist style and elements from other versions created a new one.

Despite being discussed according to kinds of symbolization, the same building can symbolize in many ways at the same time, so that there is not only one way in which buildings can participate in the process of worldmaking.

All these examples show in what specific ways buildings can contribute to the creation of worlds. Despite being discussed according to kinds of symbolization, the same building can symbolize in many ways at the same time, so that there is not only one way in which buildings can participate in the process of worldmaking. In the same way as a building can belong to several symbol systems, it can also be part of several worlds, and therefore its contribution to the making and remaking is not limited to one world, but open to many. Buildings do not constitute a world-version in their own: insofar as they are symbols within a symbol system, they are also part of a world-version and not a world in themselves. Architecture's contribution to worldmaking is very diverse and needs to be examined on a case-by-case basis. Insofar as every difference may make a difference in the work's symbolic functioning, every nuance and detail in the building can make a difference in the making of a world. One can, however, tentatively say that one of architecture's contributions to both the creation of meaning and the construction of worlds is that of achieving a superimposition of several world-versions so that the building becomes a link or joining point among them. Given architecture's three-dimensionality and realist depiction, the superimposition between fictional and non-fictional worlds may be deceptive, but on the other hand, architecture has an enormous potential to transform existing worlds by making social and political imaginaries manifest. The other main contribution is that of offering a novel way of perceiving, conceiving, and experimenting with any sort of notions, feelings, emotions, objects, materials, and spaces, as well as a novel awareness, experience, and understanding of ourselves. As Goodman says:

> **A building, more than most works, alters our environments physically; but moreover, as a work of art it may [,] through various avenues of meaning, inform and reorganize our entire experience. Like other works of art – and like scientific theories, too – it can give new insight, advance understanding, participate in our continual remaking of a world.**
>
> **(Goodman 1988: 48)**

Hence, Goodman places architecture within a philosophical context that opens up a novel way of reconceiving the architect's task. Buildings are no longer mere objects, but they have an active role in the continuous process of conveying meanings and of making and remaking worlds. Goodman's account makes us aware of relevant epistemological and metaphysical dimensions of constructing, experiencing, and interpreting buildings. Within his relativist and constructivist philosophy, where a plurality of meanings and symbol systems entails also a plurality of world-versions, each decision in designing and building brings about unexpected symbolizations, which in their turn originally contribute to the making of worlds. All these are constantly evolving depending on their symbolic and interpretative context. Architects take on an irreplaceable role as symbol-makers and world-makers in their everyday practices. Users and interpreters also contribute to the process of creating meaning and worlds as they actively engage with buildings. Both constructing and construing architecture gain a critical significance. Thinking about architecture, art, and any other symbolic endeavour from the perspective of Goodman's philosophy opens up novel ways to understand how reality is made and conceived. It prompts each of us to reconsider both our practices and how we think about them in a theoretical context that grants us the role of world-makers in a fundamental sense.

For Further Reading

My first suggestions for further reading are – as could not be otherwise – Goodman's essays on architecture: 'How Buildings Mean', and 'On Capturing Cities'. 'How Buildings Mean' is especially recommended not only because it deals with architecture, but because it contains in a nutshell most of Goodman's main philosophical conceptions; it is an excellent essay to introduce oneself in his thought. 'On Capturing Cities' is a very short text on how the symbolic grasping of a city is at the same time the making of a city.

I would further suggest continuing the reading with either *Languages of Art* or *Ways of Worldmaking*, depending on whether one is more interested in delving into Goodman's theory of symbols and the arts or in his metaphysical counterpart. In *Languages of Art*, Goodman examines the various modes of reference, deals with issues of authenticity, and investigates the technicalities of his theory of notation. Here we find also Goodman's discussion of plans and architectural renderings as well as of the identity status of buildings. *Ways of Worldmaking* is a collection of essays that includes 'Words, works, worlds' and 'The Fabrication of Facts', which deal with the process of worldmaking, and 'When Is Art?', where Goodman presents his relativist framework to understanding art.

Of Mind and Other Matters is comprised of a series of texts that Goodman wrote in response to some comments and critiques to his work. It includes clarifications and amendments to some aspects of his philosophy and concludes with an interview with Goodman. *Reconceptions in Philosophy and Other Arts and Sciences* includes 'How Buildings Mean' and other illuminating essays by Goodman and Elgin that take the theory of symbols and worldmaking as their conceptual framework and propose a third stage in their thought: that of reconceiving and rethinking philosophy and other disciplines such as architecture, music, literature, or psychology to achieve a comprehensive theory that includes all sorts of understanding. Goodman's other works do not deal with architecture or aesthetics, but for those interested in knowing more about his philosophy, I would suggest reading *Fact, Fiction, and Forecast* and learning about the so-called 'grue' paradox and the problem of induction. A deeper philosophical background is required to delve into *Problems and Projects* and *The Structure of Appearance*.

There is an extensive secondary bibliography on Goodman that ranges from introductory to highly specialized works. I would recommend Elgin's works (Elgin 1983, 1997a and 1997b) for both a thorough discussion and a developing of Goodman's thought. To know more about the theory of symbols, I suggest reading some of Cassirer's and Scheffler's works (Cassirer 1944 and Scheffler 1997). There is only a handful of works dealing with Goodman and architecture in English, none of them geared at an architectural audience, but rather to a specialized philosophical one (Mitias 1994; Paetzold 1997; Lagueux 1998; Fisher 2000; Capdevila-Werning 2009, 2011, 2013).

Bibliography

Allen, S. (2009) 'Mapping the Intangible' in S. Allen *Practice: Architecture, Technique + Representation*. London: Routledge, expanded 2nd edn, 41–69.

Amela, V. A. (1986) 'Inaugurado en Barcelona el pabellón alemán de Mies van der Rohe con la presencia de su hija', *La Vanguardia*, 3 June, 52.

Aristotle (1993) *Posterior Analytics*, translated and commented by Jonathan Barnes, 2nd edn, Oxford: Clarendon Press.

Bhatt, R. (ed.) (2013) *Rethinking Aesthetics. The Role of Body in Design*, London: Routledge.

Capdevila-Werning, R. (2009) 'Nelson Goodman's Autographic-Allographic Distinction in Architecture: Mies van der Rohe's Barcelona Pavilion' in G. Ernst, J. Steinbrenner and O. Scholz (eds) *From Logic to Art. Themes from Nelson Goodman*, Frankfurt: Ontos, 269–91.

— (2011) 'Can Buildings Quote?', *The Journal of Aesthetics and Art Criticism. Special Issue on the Aesthetics of Architecture*, 69: 115–24.

— (2013) 'From Buildings to Architecture' in R. Bhatt (ed.), *Re-thinking Aesthetics: Role of the Body in Design*, London: Routledge, 85–99.

Carlson, A. (2000) 'Existence, location, and function: the appreciation of architecture', in A. Carlson, *Aesthetics and the Environment. The Appreciation of Nature, Art, and Architecture*, New York: Routledge, 194–215.

Carter, C. (2000) 'A Tribute to Nelson Goodman', *The Journal of Aesthetics and Art Criticism* 58: 251–3.

Cassirer, E. (1944) An Essay on Man: An Introduction to a Philosophy of Human Culture, New Haven: Yale University Press.

Ching, F. D. K. (1995) *A Visual Dictionary of Architecture*, New York: Wiley & Sons.

D'Orey, C. (1999) *A Exemplificaçâo na Arte. Um Estudo sobre Nelson Goodman*, Lisboa: Fundaçâo para a Ciência e a Tecnologia.

Danto, A. (1964) 'The Artworld', *The Journal of Philosophy*, 61–19: 571–84.

— (1981) *The Transfiguration on the Commonplace*, Cambridge, MA: Harvard University Press.

Davidson, D. (1978) 'What Metaphors Mean', *Critical Inquiry,* 5–1: 31–47.

Dickie, G. (1977) *Art and the Aesthetic: An Institutional Analysis*, Ithaca: Cornell University Press.

— (1984) *The Art Circle: A Theory of Art*, New York: Haven.

Elgin, C. Z. (1983) *With Reference to Reference*, Indianapolis: Hackett.

— (1996) 'Metaphor and Reference', in Z. Radman (ed.) *From a Metaphorical Point of View*, Berlin: Walter de Gruyter, 53–72.

— (1997a) *Between the Absolute and the Arbitrary*, Ithaca: Cornell University Press.

— (1997b) *Considered Judgment*, Princeton: Princeton University Press.

— (2000) 'Worldmaker: Nelson Goodman 1906–1998', *Journal for General Philosophy of Science* 31: 1–18.

— (2010) 'Telling Instances' in R. Frigg and M. C. Hunter (eds) *Beyond Mimesis and Convention, Boston Studies in the Philosophy and History of Science* 262: 1–17.

Elgin, C. Z., Scheffler, I. and Schwartz, R. (1999) 'Nelson Goodman 1906–1998', *Proceedings and Addresses of the American Philosophical Association* 72–5: 206–8.

Fisher, S. (2000) 'Architectural Notation and Computer Aided Design', *The Journal of Aesthetics and Art Criticism,* 58: 273–89.

Fogelin, R. J. (1988) *Figuratively Speaking*, New Haven: Yale.

Genette, G. (1997) *The Work of Art. Immanence and Transcendence*, trans. G. M. Goshgarian, Ithaca: Cornell University Press.

Goodman, N. (1951) *The Structure of Appearance*, Cambridge: Harvard University Press, 2nd edn 1966, Indianapolis: Bobbs-Merrill, 3rd edn 1977, Boston: Reidel.

— (1955) *Fact, Fiction, Forecast*, Indianapolis: Bobbs-Merrill, 4th edn 1983, Cambridge, MA: Harvard University Press.

— (1968) *Languages of Art. An Approach to a Theory of Symbols*, Indianapolis: Bobbs-Merrill, 2nd edn 1976, Indianapolis: Hackett.

— (1972) *Problems and Projects*, Indianapolis: Bobbs-Merrill.

— (1978) *Ways of Worldmaking*, Indianapolis: Hackett.

— (1979) 'Metaphor as Moonlighting', *Critical Inquiry,* 6–1: 125–30.

— (1984) *Of Mind and Other Matters*, Cambridge, MA: Harvard University Press.

— (1985), 'How Buildings Mean', *Critical Inquiry* 11–4: 642–53.

— (1991) 'On Capturing Cities', *Journal of Aesthetic Education* 25–1: 5–9. First published in G. Teyssot (ed.), *World cities and the future of the metropoles / XVII Triennale di Milano*, Vol. 1, Milano: Electa, 69–71.

Goodman, N. and Elgin C. Z. (1988) *Reconceptions in Philosophy and Other Arts and Sciences*, Indianapolis: Hackett.

Graaf, R. de (2008) 'Manifesto for Simplicity   Serpentine Gallery Manifesto Marathon', 19 October 2008. Available HTTP: www.oma.nl (accessed 10 November, 2011).

Harvard College. Class of 1928 (1978) *Fiftieth anniversary report*, Cambridge, MA: Crimson Printing Co.

Hellman, G. (1977) 'Symbol Systems and Artistic Styles', *The Journal of Aesthetics and Art Criticism*, 35: 279–92.

Iseminger, G. (ed.) (1992) *Intention and Interpretation*, Philadelphia: Temple University Press.

Kieran, M. (ed.) (2006) *Contemporary Debates in Aesthetics and the Philosophy of Art*, Malden, MA: Blackwell.

Lagueux, M. (1998) 'Nelson Goodman and Architecture', Assemblage, 35: 18–35.

Lang, B. (ed.) (1987) *The Concept of Style*, Ithaca: Cornell University Press.

Libeskind, D. and Binet, H. (1999) *Jewish Museum Berlin*, S.I.: G + B Arts International.

Light, A. and Smith, J. A. (2005) *Aesthetics of Everyday Life*, New York: Columbia University Press.

Marx, K. (1990) *Capital. A Critique of Political Economy*, Vol. 1, trans. B. Fowkes, London: Penguin. 1st edn, Hamburg: Verlag Otto von Meissner, 1867.

Mitias. M. (1994) 'Expression in Architecture' in M. Mitias (ed.), *Philosophy and Architecture*, Amsterdam: Rodopi, 87–107.

— (1990) 'The Aesthetic Experience of the Architectural Work', *Journal of Aesthetic Education*, 33: 61–77.

Moos, S. von (1987) *Venturi, Rauch & Scott Brown: Buildings and Projects*, New York: Rizzoli.

Paetzold, H. (1997) *The symbolic language of culture, fine arts and architecture. Consequences of Cassirer and Goodman, Three Trondheim Lectures*, Trondheim: FF Edition.

Pevsner, N. (1963) *An Outline of European Architecture,* 7th edn, Harmondsworth: Penguin Books. 1st edn, London: Pelican, 1943.

Rasmussen, S. E. (1959) *Experiencing Architecture*, Cambridge, MA: Massachusetts Institute of Technology Press.

Ross, S. (1981) 'Art and Allusion', *The Journal of Aesthetics and Art Criticism*, 40: 59–70.

Rush, F. (2009) *On Architecture*, London: Routledge.

Saito, Y. (2007) *Everyday Aesthetics*, New York: Oxford University Press.

Scheffler, I. (1997) Symbolic worlds: art, science, language, ritual, Cambridge: Cambridge University Press.

Scruton, R. (1979) *The Aesthetics of Architecture*, London: Meuthen.

Solà-Morales, I. de, Cirici, C. and Ramos, F. (1993) *Mies van der Rohe: Barcelona Pavilion*, Barcelona: Gustavo Gili.

Stubbs, J. H. (2009) *Time Honored. A Global View of Architectural Conservation*, Hoboken: Wiley.

Venturi, R. (1966) *Complexity and Contradiction in Architecture*, New York: Museum of Modern Art.

Vermaulen I., Brun, G. and Baumberger, Ch. (2009) 'Five Ways of (not) Defining Exemplification' in G. Ernst, J. Steinbrenner and O. Scholz (eds) *From Logic to Art. Themes from Nelson Goodman*, Frankfurt: Ontos, 219–50.

Yanal, R. J. (1998) 'The Institutional Theory of Art', in M. Kelly (ed.) *Encyclopedia of Aesthetics*, London: Oxford Art Online Online. Available HTTP: http://www.oxfordartonline.com/subscriber/article/opr/t234/e0292 (accessed 11 January 2010).

Young, J. E. (2000) *At Memory's Edge. After-Images of the Holocaust in Contemporary Art and Architecture*, New Haven: Yale University Press.

Index

Numbers in **bold** type indicate illustrations

absolutism 14, 17, 18

aesthetic, aesthetics 1, 5, 6, 78;
cognitive role 6; everyday 28;
experience 7, 23–30, 110;
symptoms of the 7, 77–9

allographic 7, 34, 80–4, 86, 87–99;
definition of 81–2

allusion 7, 31, 32, 65–9, 70, 111;
definition of 65; ironic 69

ambiguity 31, 33, 39, 85

analogue 37–8, 86–7; *see also* digital

analytic philosophy 1

architects as symbol-makers and
world-makers 4, 5, 6, 23, 30, 31,
48, 54, 100, 113

architecture: aesthetic experience
of 23–9; notation of 83–7;
philosophical role of 112–13;
versus buildings 5, 9–10, 13, 21;
see also architects, arts, work of
architecture; *passim*

Aristotle 32

articulation 7, 28, 49, 53–4, 58–9,
76, 77

arts: multiple 81, 88; one-stage
89; public 27–8; singular 81,
88; two-stage 89; *see also*

architecture, drama, etching,
literature, music, painting,
sculpture, work of art

attenuation 33, 36, 37, 78

authenticity 80, 81, 92, 114; *see also*
identity

autographic 7, 80–3, 87–99;
definition of 81

Bach, J. S. 69, 82

Barcelona Pavilion 48, 50, 80, 93–9,
94, 109

Baroque space vs Renaissance space
110

Bathing Pavilion 34–6, **35, 36**

beauty 6

belief 3, 103

Benjamin, Walter 1

Bernini 71

Borromini 49

brutalist architecture 50

buildings versus architecture 5, 9–10,
13, 21

Ca' del Duca Palace 44, **45**

Calatrava, Santiago 20

Carpenter Center 76

Cathedral of Barcelona 25, 27

Centre Georges Pompidou 49–50, 53, 76

chain of reference 41, 55, 65–7, 69; *see also* metaphor

character 32–3, 34; character-indifference 33

Cinderella Castle 42, 89–90, 99, 106

classification 43, 56, 82, 87, 93; antecedent 82, 87

cognition 6, 24, 25, 29, 43, 56; *see also* comprehension, epistemology, knowledge, understanding

coherence 18, 30, 103; *see also* criteria

Columns of Constantine 71

compliance 33, 78

comprehension 101, 110; *see also* understanding

Computer Aided Design (CAD) 86

conditions, necessary and sufficient 20–1, 52, 53, 54, 59, 68, 78, 95

consistency 18, 30, 103; *see also* criteria

construal 5, 6, 17, 18, 22, 23, 30, 103, 113; *see also* interpretation

constructivism 1, 4–5, 7, 10, 18, 21, 22, 23, 25, 100, 102, 113

context 18, 19–22, 27, 39, 75, 79, 113

continental philosophy 1

copy 7, 39, 40–1, 67, 70–1, 80–1, 87, 88, 93, 99, 107

Corbusier *see* Le Corbusier

correctness 15, 18, 47, 75–7; *see also* criteria, truth

criteria 7, 15, 17–18, 21, 23, 29, 30, 75–9, 102–3; identity criteria 80–3, 93; *see also* allographic, autographic

Danto, Arthur 19

deconstructivism 73, 111

Deleuze, Gilles 1

denotation 7, 32, 34, 38–45, 65–6, 105–6; in architecture 39–45; definition of 38–9; and exemplification 46; metaphorical 39, 55–7; null 38–9, 42; pictorial 40–3; verbal 39–40; *see also* model, notation, quotation, representation

denotation-as *see* representation-as

density 33, 34, 36, 37, 47; semantic 34; as symptom 77–9; syntactic 34

depiction 38–9, 41, 42, 51–2, 112; *see also* pictorial denotation, picture, representation, x-picture and picture of

Derrida, Jacques 1

description 38–9, 42, 43; *see also* verbal denotation, x-picture and picture of

diagram 35, 36, 37, 85

Dickie, George 19

differentiation 33

digital 37, 85, 86; *see also* analogue

disjointess 33, 34, 78

drama 34, 84–6

Dunmore Pavilion 40, 41, **60**, 60–1

Eiffel Tower 40–1, 48, 67, 71, 80, 107

Einstein, Albert 105

elevation *see* notation of architecture

Elgin, Catherine Z. xiv, 2, 33, 65, 114, 115

emotion 3, 6, 29, 54, 55, 58, 65, 110, 112; cognitive function of 29

Empire State Building 58

epistemology 1, 3, 5, 6, 100–2; *see also* cognition, metaphysics

essentialism 6–7, 10–14, 21, 22, 30

etching 81, 82, 90

evaluation 7, 15, 23, 54, 56, 75–7; *see also* criteria

evocation 31, 65–6

example 7–8, 47; *see also* exemplification

exemplification 7, 32, 44, 46–52, 59, 61, 62, 65–6, 69, 70, 78–9, 104, 109–10; in architecture 48–52; articulation and 49, 53–4; in the arts 47; definition of 46; denotation and 46; metaphorical 54, 57–8; as symptom 78–9; *see also* expression, model, possession

experience, aesthetic 7, 23–30, 110

expression 7, 31, 32, 51, 54–64, 65, 74, 104, 110; in architecture 59–64; definition of 54, 57–8; and metaphorical exemplification 57–8; *see also* exemplification, metaphor, possession

extension, primary and secondary 39

fact 102, 114

fake 75, 80; *see also* authenticity, identity

Fallingwater House 26

feeling *see* emotion

fiction 39, 42, 105, 106, 112; *see also* null denotation, null reference

Filarete's column 44, **45**

fit 18, 75

forgery 80, 81, 93, 99; *see also* authenticity, identity

Foucault, Michel 1

function, functioning: aesthetic 13, 16, 20, 21, 28, 78–9; practical 3, 5, 12, 28, 30, 31, 42–3, 64, 106; symbolic 5, 13, 18, 19, 20, 21, 22, 35, 36–7, 38, 70, 79, 103, 106, 108, 112; *see also* reference, symptoms of the aesthetic

functionalism 9–10, 12, 22, 30, 48

Gas Natural headquarters 39

Gaudí, Antoni 40, 41, 67; *see also* Sagrada Família

Gehry, Frank 49, 73, 74; *see also* Guggenheim Museum in Bilbao, Stata Center

German Pavilion *see* Barcelona Pavilion

Goldberg Variations 82
Goodman, Nelson **xv**; biography 2–3; main works 1–2, 117–18; summary of his thought 1–8, 21, 22, 112–13; *passim*
Gothic 25, 27, 38, 48, 49, 74; versus neo-Gothic 74
Graduate House at the University of Toronto 39–40
Grand Central Station 108
grue 115
Guggenheim Museum in Bilbao 48, 77
Guggenheim Museum in New York 108

Hadid, Zaha 48
Heidegger, Martin 1
Hogwarts Castle 39
Hokusai 35

identity 7, 34, 41, 80–99; *see also* allographic, authenticity, autographic, copy, fake, forgery, reconstruction, restoration
implementation 20
institutionalism 7, 10, 19–21, 30
intention 7, 14–19, 21, 68
intentionalism 7, 10, 14–19, 30
interpretation 4–7, 13, 14–19, 21–3, 24, 30, 38, 47, 54, 55, 56, 58, 64, 67, 68, 100, 112; constitutive role of 21–3; *see also* aesthetic experience, construal, criteria, interpreter
interpreter 18, 19, 113

irony 4, 41, 69, 103, 107, 111
irrealism 1, 5; *see also* realism

Jefferson, Thomas 68, 111
Jewish Museum 18, 61–4, **62**, 110
John Hancock Tower 48, 53, 77
Jordy, William H. 49
Juliet's House 42–3, 106

Kahn, Louis 16, 50
knowledge 3, 38, 67; *see also* cognition, understanding
Koolhaas, Rem 88; *see also* Office of Metropolitan Architecture (OMA)

label 38, 39, 46, 55, 56, 57, 59, 66, 67; *see also* literal, metaphor, property
Le Corbusier 76; *see also* Carpenter Center, Maison du Brésil, Villa Citrohan, Villa Savoye, Villa Stein-de-Monzie
Leers Weinzapfel Associates 50, **51**; *see also* Science Center
Lerner Hall at Columbia University 44, **44**
Libeskind, Daniel 61, 62, 63; *see also* Jewish Museum
Lincoln Cathedral 9
literal 39, 51, 54–7, 58, 59, 60, 65, 66, 69, 70, 78; *see also* label, metaphor, property
literature 71, 81, 82, 84, 96
Low Memorial Library at Columbia University 68, 70, 111

MacAllister, John 16
Maison du Brésil 76, 110
mark 32, 33, 34
Marx, Karl 9
May, Ernst 106
McKim, Mead, and White 68; *see also* Low Memorial Library
meaning *see* cognition, reference, symbol
Meegeren, H. van 75
metaphor 31, 39, 51, 54–8, 65, 66, 70; and truth 56–7; *see also* expression, label, literal, metaphorical exemplification, property
metaphysics 5, 6, 100–2
Michelangelo 68
Mies van der Rohe, Ludwig 80, 93, 109; *see also* Barcelona Pavilion, Seagram Building
model 4, 20, **35**, 36, 37, 38, 41, 46, 47, 76, 86; denoting 36–7, 38, 41; exemplifying 46, 47, 76, 86; *see also* denotation, exemplification
Modern Art Museum of Fort Worth 39
Morningside Campus at Columbia University 72
multiple arts 81, 88
music 24, 26, 33, 34, 59, 69, 76, 80, 81–2, 84–5, 96, 97, 100–1; *see also* score

necessary condition *see* conditions, necessary and sufficient

neo-Gothic 74
Neuschwanstein Castle 43
notation 7, 32, 33–4, 37, 39, 78, 81–7, 89, 90, 95, 96, 97, 98, 99, 114; architecture's 7, 33–4, 39, 83–7, 89, 90, 95, 97, 98; practical function of 34, 83; theoretical function of 34, 83–4; *see also* allographic, denotation, identity
notational scheme 33–4, 84, 85–7
notational system 33–4, 82, 83, 84, 85–7
Notre-Dame in Paris 109
novelty 55, 76, 77; *see also* criteria
null reference *see* reference, null; *see also* null denotation, fiction

Office of Metropolitan Architecture (OMA) 88, 99
one-stage art 89
ontology 22, 23; *see also* metaphysics
original 7, 40, 41, 67, 80–1, 88, 92, 93, 94, 95, 97, 98, 99, 107, 108–9; *see also* authenticity, copy, identity, replica

painting 22, 24, 25, 26, 27, 36, 40, 42, 78, 80, 81, 82, 90
Palladio 48, 68, 100; *see also* Villa Rotonda
Pantheon 68, 70–1, 111
Parthenon 40–1, 80, 83, 88
perception 24–5, 29, 30, 74, 104, 105

performance 2, 24, 82, 84, 85

Pergamon Altar 89–90

Pevsner, Nikolaus 9

philosophy, analytic and continental 1

picture 38; *see also* pictorial
denotation, representation,
x-picture versus picture-of

plans *see* notation of architecture

pleasure 29

pluralism 1, 5, 7, 22, 30

Poblenou 15

Porta Pia 68

possession 46, 47, 48, 51, 52, 53, 57,
58, 60, 67, 72, 76, 97; *see also*
exemplification, literal, metaphor,
property

practice, precedent 99; *see also*
classification

pragmatism 22

preservation 107–9; *see also*
restoration, reconstruction

projectibility 76

property 46, 55, 57, 58, 59, 60, 64,
66, 67–8, 73; essential 10–11;
see also exemplification, label

quotation 31, 39, 43–5, **44**, **45**, 103

RCR Arquitectes xiv, 34, **35**, **36**; *see
also* Bathing Pavilion

realism 42, 106, 112; *see also* irrealism

reality 1, 3, 5, 42, 43, 102, 104, 105,
113

realm 32, 33; *see also* field of
reference

reconstruction 7, 80, 93–9, 107–9

reference 4, 7, 13, 31–75; chain of,
41, 55, 65–7, 69; explication of
13, 31–2; fictive 39, 42, 105,
106, 112; field of 32, 33; null
38–9, 42, 105; *see also* allusion,
denotation, exemplification,
expression, realm, style, symbol,
variation; *passim*

relativism 1, 5, 6, 7, 17–18, 21, 23
100, 112; constructive 18, 21,
23, 100; radical 17, 18, 21; *see
also* absolutism

relativity 5, 73, 75

Renaissance space versus Baroque
space 110

repleteness 35, 36, 78, 79; as
symptom 78–9; *see also*
attenuation

replica 43, 44, 81, 84, 88, 93–8;
syntactic 43–4; *see also*
authenticity, allographic,
autographic, copy, identity

representation 35, 40–3, 60–1,
67, 70, 106; *see also* pictorial
denotation, depiction, picture,
representation-as, x-picture
versus picture of

representation-as 43

resemblance 41–2, 43

restoration 7, 43, 80, 90–3, 99,
107–9

Rietveld, Gerrit 49

rightness 7, 14, 17, 18, 19, 21, 23,
30, 75–7, 100–3

Rinehart, David 16

Romanesque 15, 25, 74, 90–2, **91**

Rossi, Aldo 44, **45**; *see also*
Wilhelmstrasse apartments

Rotunda 68, 111

Sagrada Família 40, 41, 67

Salk Institute 16

Saltbox houses 9, 11, 12, 79

sample 46–7, 78, 86; from the sea 47

Sant'Ignazio di Loyola 67

Sant'Ivo alla Sapienza 49

Sant Pere de Rodes 90–2, **91**

Santa Maria del Mar 25

Scarpa, Carlo 50

scheme 32, 33–4, 84, 85–7; *see also*
notational scheme

Schröder House 49

Science Center at Harvard University
50, **51**, 52, 53, 76, 77, 110

score 34, 81–2, 84–6, 96–7

script 34, 82, 84–6, 97

sculpture 27, 40, 42, 81, 82, 90

Seagram Building 28, 48

section *see* notation of architecture

signature 73, 88

singular art 81, 88

site-specificity 26, 89–90

sketch 34, **35**, 36, 37, 38, 85

Sleeping Beauty Castle 42, 43, 106

Solomonic columns 71, 72

Son Goku 67, 105

Sorites paradox 84

Soufflot, Jacques-Germain 68

Stalin's Museum 44

Stata Center at the Massachusetts
Institute of Technology 49, 52,
73

Sturgis, Katharine 2

style 4, 7, 16, 25, 32, 38, 65, 67,
68, 69, 70, 72, 73–5; versus
signature 73

sufficient condition *see* conditions,
necessary and sufficient

suggestion 67–8

Sydney Opera House 17, 40, 48, 67,
105

symbol 4–6, 7, 10, 12–14, 21, 30,
31–2; aesthetic 13–14, 20, 21,
30, 77–9; *see also* allusion,
denotation, exemplification,
expression, realm, reference,
style, variation; *passim*

symbolization *see* reference

symbol-making 4, 5, 23, 30, 113; *see
also* architects as symbol-makers

symbol scheme *see* scheme

symbol system *see* system

symptoms of the aesthetic 7, 77–9

system 4, 6, 7, 14, 16, 17, 18, 22,
30, 31–8, 39, 43, 47–8, 52,
54, 56–7, 58, 74–5, 100–1,
102, 103, 105, 112; *see also*
notational system

Taj Mahal 9, 11, 12, 38, 58, 87, 90,
99

Temple of Augustus **26**, 27

Temple of Salomon 71

text 78, 81, 82, 84

The Pineapple *see* Dunmore Pavilion
Theseus, paradox of the ship of 92
Tower of Babel 38–9
tract housing 41, 80, 83, 87, 88, 99
Trajan's Column 71
truth 56, 75, 102; *see also* rightness
Tschumi, Bernard 44, **44**
TWA terminal 42
two-stage art 89

understanding 3, 4, 6, 29, 31, 38, 46,
48, 56, 76, 101–3, 105, 112; *see
also* cognition, epistemology

validity 3, 15, 16, 17, 19, 41, 103;
see also criteria, rightness
Vall de Boí, Romanesque churches
15, 25
Vanna Venturi House 66, 67, 68, 69,
111
variation 7, 32, 65, 69–72, 103, 111;
in architecture 70–2; in music
69–70
Venturi, Robert 66, 69; *see also*
Vanna Venturi House
Vermeer, Johannes 75
version *see* world-version
Vierzehnheiligen Basilica 59
Villa Citrohan 76
Villa Rotonda 48, 68, 100–1, 110,
111

Villa Savoye 76
Villa Stein-de-Monzie 76
Viollet-le-Duc 109

what versus when 5, 6–7, 9–22, 30
Wilhelmstrasse apartments 44, **45**
work of architecture 5, 9–21, 47–8;
see also work of art
work of art 5, 9, 12, 13, 16, 17, 19,
20, 28, 29, 77, 81, 112; *see also*
aesthetic symbol, sample from
the sea
world 4–7, 23, 30, 31, 100–4,
112–13; fictional 105–6, 112;
see also world-version
world-version 5, 23, 29, 31, 100–13;
see also world
worldmaking 4, 5, 7, 48, 100–13;
architectural ways of 104–12;
definition of 103–4, ways of,
103–4; *see also* architects as
world-makers
Wright, Frank Lloyd 26; *see also*
Fallingwater House, Guggenheim
Museum in New York

x-picture and picture of 42–3, 105,
106

Zumthor, Peter 50